Practical Goat Keeping

PRACTICAL GOAT KEEPING

Alan Mowlem

The Crowood Press

First published in 2001 by
The Crowood Press Ltd
Ramsbury, Marlborough
Wiltshire SN8 2HR

British Library Cataloguing-in-Publication Data
A catalogue record for this book is available from the British Library.

ISBN 1 86126 389 9

Illustration Acknowledgements
The photographs in Chapter 10 were kindly supplied by Hilary Mathews. All other photographs are by the author.

Line drawings by David Fisher.

Designed and edited by Focus Publishing, Sevenoaks, Kent

Printed and bound in Great Britain by Antony Rowe, Chippenham, Wiltshire

Contents

Introduction ——————————

The goat, along with the dog, was almost certainly the first animal to be domesticated. Those who become involved with goats soon realize that they are perfect candidates for this role – although being goats, this is always on their terms. Their early history in the UK is not known, but evidence suggests that they have been used here since the time of the Roman occupation. They have always been popular amongst smallholders, but have been regarded with some suspicion by the larger, more commercial farmer. However, more recent changes in the fortunes of farming have focused interest on a number of alternative enterprises, and it is now possible to find farms with more than 1,000 milking goats.

Although this growth of very large goat farms has happened relatively recently, there has always been a keen interest in smaller-scale goat keeping, where the motives are primarily the pleasure of keeping and breeding this unique animal. This usually leads to more products than one family can use, and thus a small-scale farming enterprise is born. This book is intended to be a guide for those keeping goats on a small scale, although a great deal of the information will of course apply to the goat in any situation, and so may be of interest to anyone keeping them.

1 The Goat: Characteristics and Breeds

Goats are often compared with other farm animals, and as a result it soon becomes apparent that they share many aspects of husbandry with them, particularly sheep and cows. On the other hand, it is difficult to find any similarities in their behaviour. Goats are inquisitive, active and possibly intelligent animals – 'possibly' because it is difficult to rate intelligence objectively, without conducting some form of test. Certainly their inquisitiveness gives an impression of intelligence: for instance, they will thoroughly investigate any environment which is new to them, whether this be field, paddock, pen or shed. By way of comparison, when sheep are put into a fresh field they normally start eating as soon as they pass through the gate. Goats, on the other hand, will rush around the perimeter, clamber up on the fence to reach overhanging branches, and will quickly find any weak points in the perimeter boundary and break into the next field if they possibly can. Inside a building they will investigate anything within reach – and this is considerable, because they will habitually stand up on their hindlegs, supporting themselves by bracing their front legs against a wall or suchlike, and a full-grown goat will be able to reach at least 2m (6½ft) above ground level. In fact anything that will not withstand being investigated by chewing will be vulnerable, including electric cable, fittings, taps and hosepipes.

Some goats acquire the habit of chewing wood, and can cause a great deal of damage to parts of buildings such as doors and window frames. Not all goats do this,

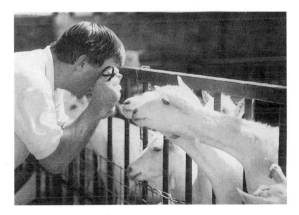

Goats are inquisitive, active and possibly intelligent animals!

By standing up on their hind legs adult goats can reach to 2m (6½ft).

however, and with luck will be quite content housed in a relatively flimsy wooden shed.

Not all aspects of a goat's character are negative. They are extremely friendly animals, and seem to enjoy attention. Goats kept in small numbers, and those that have been hand-reared as on dairy units, grow up to be completely 'people-friendly'; they will follow their carer anywhere, and will always come across to investigate whatever he or she is doing. This makes any task that involves handling them relatively easy. Further-more they are easy to catch if they are accustomed to being petted rather than chased; and when they *are* caught, they usually stand still with the minimum of restraint. Having said that, if they sense that you want to catch them and they don't want to be, they can be just *the* most difficult of animals to corner. Anyone with more than just one or two goats is well advised to feed them each day, even if they are out to pasture and do not necessarily need it, because once goats learn to recognize a feed bucket or bag they can usually be led almost anywhere! If goats trained in this way ever manage to get out

An opportunistic goat in a show tent helping itself to feed in a neighbouring pen.

from their pen or paddock they can usually be led back to where they belong by someone rattling a food bucket or bag! This technique is also useful if one goat in a group needs to be caught: it is relatively easy to grab hold of it if they are all crowding round to get at the food. The friendliness of goats makes them very pleasant animals to own or to work with, and they can be just as rewarding, if not more so, than any dog. However, this friendliness towards their human companions is not always manifested amongst themselves, and in a group situation they can be very spiteful to any individual they take a dislike to. Because of this, running unfamiliar adult animals together is no easy matter, and there will be a lot of bullying in this situation until a 'pecking order' has been established. And if any one goat is continually bullied it can suffer a great deal of stress, to the point, sometimes, of making it ill. Because of this, anyone wanting to build up a herd would be well advised to do so with young weanlings, as these will not show the same aggressive tendencies, and can usually be mixed without problems. If older goats are mixed in together they need plenty of floor and feeding space until they have accepted each other and have established a hierarchy. Goats with horns are always much more difficult, and are more likely to bully than those without.

All this adds up to an animal with an individual character: in short, no two goats will behave the same, and thus a group of twenty goats will behave as twenty individuals – unlike a group of twenty cows or sheep, which tend to behave as a single group.

WHY KEEP GOATS?

If the reader has not been put off the whole idea of goats by now, the next step is to consider how to become established as a goat keeper. The first decision to make is what sort of goat to have, and the choice in the UK is the same as in practically any other country, namely between dairy, fibre or meat. Inevitably this depends on *why* you want to keep goats, and what you hope to get out of goat-keeping, usually this is for one of three reasons: you want them as pets; or for the science of breeding and breed improvement; or for their products, which may mean they are to be the main source of income, or just a self-supporting hobby.

The natural friendliness of goats makes them ideal pets for anyone with suitable facilities to keep them. The minimum requirements are a paddock or yard in which they can exercise freely, and a shelter which will keep them dry when it is raining and free of draughts when the winter winds are blowing. These aspects will be covered fully in the next chapter. A farm or smallholding usually has some buildings which would be suitable for goats with a minimum of alteration.

One of the most important prerequisites for goat keeping is total commitment on the part of the goat keeper: like any animal, they are a big responsibility and a considerable tie, meaning that it is really not possible just to up and leave them and go off on holiday, for instance, unless a reliable relief goat 'sitter' is available. Furthermore, goats can quite readily take up a totally disproportionate amount of the goat keeper's time, as compared to other domesticated animals, and this level of attention requires real committment on the part of their keeper. Anyone used to the relatively undemanding cow may well be in for a surprise, if not a shock, when they find out how demanding goats can be. And those with no experience at all of goat keeping would be wise to visit someone who has got some goats to acquire some idea of what is involved, and to see how someone else has approached the various aspects of their husbandry requirements.

The next thing to consider is what breed, or breeds of goat you want to keep. There are well over 200 identifiable breeds of goat in the world, with some thirteen in the UK. There are also many cross-breds, a large number of which have very distinct colour markings, giving them the appearance of other breeds.

DAIRY BREEDS

Saanen

The Saanen and its derivatives comprise the most popular dairy breed. The pure Saanen originates from the Saanen Valley in the south of the Canton Berne in Switzerland, but it is also found in the Simmental Valley where it is known as the Gessenay goat. The hair of the Saanen is always white, though sometimes it has black markings on its skin, in particular around the nose, ears and udder. The coat is usually a little rough, sometimes with a long 'skirt' of hair growing around the back legs. The average weight for a female would be 55–65kg (120–140lb), and milk yields up to 2,000kg (4,410lb) per annum can be achieved.

Most of the pure Saanens in the UK derive from an importation from Switzerland in the 1920s, though advances in artifical insemination technology have made it possible for semen from Saanens in Switzerland to be imported into the UK in recent times.

A British Saanen showing the all-white colouration.

British Saanen

These goats are the result of cross-breeding Saanens with other breeds to give an improved Saanen type which the British Goat Society recognized as a breed in 1925.

They are very similar to pure Saanens – indeed it is often difficult to tell them apart. They tend to be a little larger, with females weighing up to 70kg (154lb) and males 90–100kg (198–220lb). They have surpassed the parent breed in terms of milking performance, and now hold the world record for the highest annual milk yield from a goat: this was from Dawnus Chloe, who produced a yield of 3,583kg (7,900lb) in 1998.

This level of milk production would not be achieved in a large commercial herd, but it does indicate that herd averages of over 1,000kg (2,205lb) of milk per year should be possible.

Both Saanen breeds are relatively placid, making them particularly suitable for commercial dairy farms.

A British Toggenburg is light brown with characteristic white markings on the head, feet and tail.

Toggenburg

Another Swiss breed, that comes from the Canton of St Gallen. They are light brown, with distinctive white markings on their head and legs, and on the rump around the tail. They usually have quite a long, rough coat, often with a 'skirt' of long hair hanging around their legs. They may be horned or polled. They can produce milk yields similar to the Saanen, and are of similar temperament, although some would argue they are a little more 'excitable' than Saanens.

British Toggenburg

These goats have a similar history to British Saanens in as much as they originate from cross-breeding with Toggenburgs at around the end of the nineteenth and beginning of the twentieth century; they were accepted as a breed in their own right in 1925. They are larger than pure Toggenburgs, and produce more milk of slightly better compositional quality than that from the British Saanen. Many commercial herds have a mixture of these two breeds.

British Alpines have similar markings to the British Toggenburg but their coat is glossy black.

British Alpine

Another breed with Swiss origins. Although it has markings similar to the Swiss Bundner Strhlenziege, it is only very distantly related to it. It was in fact created from cross-breeding during the early twentieth century. It has a shiny black coat with white markings around the face, legs and tail, in much the same pattern as the Toggenburg. British Alpines can produce high milk yields, but do not average quite as much as British Saanens or British Toggenburgs.

Anglo-Nubians showing the characteristic 'Roman' nose and large, droopy ears.

Anglo-Nubian

This breed originates from the crossing of Middle Eastern and Indian breeds with the then indigenous English breed at the end of the nineteenth century. The most characteristic features of this goat, as compared with all the other breeds in the UK, are their long pendulous ears and large 'Roman' nose. They are big goats, the females weighing around 70kg (154lb) and the males 100kg (220lb). They can be of any colour, though dark brown with a black stripe along their back is the most common. This is the colour of the English goat. Anglo-Nubians do not produce as much milk as the 'Swiss' breeds, although some individuals give impressive yields. However, their milk is of much better quality than most other breeds, with a much higher content of both fat and protein.

In temperament they are generally more 'excitable', and in large herds they do not seem to mix well with other breeds – in commercial herds they perform best when they make up the majority. They have a longer breeding season than most other breeds, probably a trait inherited from their tropical origins.

Golden Guernseys usually have quite a long coat which may be golden brown through to chestnut brown.

Golden Guernsey

As the name suggests, this breed originates from the Channel Islands. Although numbers are increasing, they are classified as a rare breed by the Rare Breeds Survival Trust in the UK. Their colour ranges from sandy brown to a rich reddish brown, and they usually have a fairly long coat, often with a skirt of hair around their legs. They are gentle goats and are possibly more suitable for keeping in small numbers as they do not seem to mix well with other breeds in large herds. Some individual Golden Guernseys produce a lot of milk, but they do not average the large yields produced by the 'Swiss' breeds. It is quite likely that selective breeding will raise the average performance of this breed.

14

A young English goat at the Bucks Goat Centre, showing the typical black markings along the back and on the legs.

English

This once common breed had disappeared by the 1940s, but fortunately enough characteristics survived amongst the cross-bred goat population of the United Kingdom for it to be 'recreated'. These goats can be multi-coloured, but typically they are brown with black markings along the back and around the ears and legs, very much like the alpine goats of other European countries.

Cross-breeding the main 'Swiss' breeds in some of the larger commercial herds creates English-type colour markings. The recreated English breed is hardy, and performs well on feed of relatively low nutritional value, making it a useful smallholder's goat.

15

A rare Bagot female showing the characteristic black head and shoulders.

Bagot

The ancestry of these rare goats can be traced back to the fourteenth century when they were first established at Blythfield Hall in Staffordshire. They probably share a common ancestry with the Swiss Schwarzhal breed, which they resemble with their long white coat and black head and shoulders. They do not seem to have any commercial value, but like all minority breeds, it is essential that they are preserved in case they have traits that may be considered useful by future generations.

A Pygmy female with twin kids.

Pygmy Goat

These are more accurately called West African Dwarf goats, and can be found in a number of countries around the 'bulge' of West Africa. They are true dwarves, with a mature bodyweight of around 25kg (55lb).

They can be almost any colour, but most are black, brown or grey and white, or a combination of these. They are great characters and make good – albeit cunning! – pets; they are popular on open farms where children visit.

17

A young Angora female whose fine ringlets indicate fine mohair.

FIBRE BREEDS

Angora

This breed originates from Turkey, although nowadays angora goats are farmed in their largest numbers in South Africa. Their hair is called 'mohair', and is used in the manufacture of a wide range of products such as carpets, curtains, upholstery velours, suiting and skirt materials and knitting yarns. They are normally white, but darker colours do exist. Their long, lustrous hair means they are often mistaken for sheep by those who are unfamiliar with them. They were imported into the UK in the early 1980s from New Zealand and Tasmania, and since then, further imports of South African and Texan types have been made, resulting in some very good goats. The fall in mohair value during this period has meant that not many people have been encouraged to farm them on a large scale. However, some breeders have persisted, many adding value to their own mohair by processing it, and now the overall value of mohair is increasing again.

Windsor Whites, descended from imported cashmere goats.

Cashmere

There is no 'cashmere' breed of goat as such, but there are goats in a number of regions that are kept specifically for cashmere production.

Cashmere is a soft under-hair that grows as an insulating layer beneath the main outer hair of many types of goat. If not harvested by combing, it is moulted out in the spring and can be seen hanging on fences and bushes in areas where these goats are kept.

Even well bred dairy goats will produce some cashmere if kept in relatively cold environments. Toggenburgs, for example, will shed quite significant amounts of this hair, particularly if they spend a lot of the winter outside.

A feral goat in Scotland looks at the photographer before 'melting' into the undergrowth.

Feral Goats

There are still some herds of feral goats in the remoter parts of the British Isles and Ireland. They originate from those that have escaped from domestication in previous centuries, and in certain areas quite large herds can be seen. They are usually of mixed colours, though some in more isolated areas still resemble the goats from which they originate.

Certain herds have most interesting origins, and in recent years some have been the focus of interest for possible cashmere production. The rare Windsor White goats that roam on the Great Orme peninsular in North Wales originate from cashmere goats brought to England in 1823.

A Boer male showing impressive conformation and characteristic markings around the head.

MEAT BREEDS

Boer

Although throughout the world more goats are used for their meat than anything else, there is only one breed that has been developed specifically for meat production: the Boer, from South Africa. Over the past forty years these indigenous goats have been carefully bred to improve carcass conformation and meat yield, resulting in an amazing goat that is unlike any other breed. The best males in South Africa will weigh in excess of 150kg (330lb) and are most impressive creatures. Boer goats are always white, with reddish brown heads and shoulders. They have long, pendulous ears, but do not have the extremely bent nose associated with Anglo Nubians.

This breed has been imported into the UK, and, although not as good as the best to be found in South Africa, they are of great interest to those hoping to see growth of the goat meat market in the UK. It is possible that in time Boer goats may be used to cross with dairy breeds, in the same way that beef bulls are used on dairy cows.

WHICH BREED TO CHOOSE?

The choice of breed will depend on the aspirations of the goat keeper. Some like to see colour, some are attracted by the distinctive looks of Anglo-Nubians, some just want a docile pet, and some may be interested in crafting fine garments from their own mohair or cashmere.

The sex of the goats to be purchased must also be considered. There is always a surplus of unwanted male kids, mainly because there is very little demand for goat meat in the UK. However, would-be goat keepers are strongly advised not to buy an entire male kid, however appealing it may be, because they grow up into large and very smelly animals and do not make good pets at all. Castrated males are quite different: certainly they do grow very large, but apart from this they make almost ideal pets. They usually grow up to be very friendly, but without the characteristic smell of an entire male, and of course they do not need milking.

Castrated males are the favourites for training to harness. The Harness Goat Society has revived the tradition of goats pulling small carts and wagons, particularly for children, and usually delight the crowds when they put on a display at shows and suchlike.

Female goats have their problems, too. For instance, it is not at all unusual for the udder of unmated females to develop to the point where they need milking. These females are usually called maiden milkers, and anyone buying a female kid must realize that they may be faced with twice daily milking, even though they do not intend breeding from it.

Goats are not available in the same way as for other farm livestock, and there is not a regular trade in goats through livestock markets – in fact, some will not handle goats at all. For those wishing to start up a commercial dairy enterprise,

The Choice of Breeds in Great Britain

Dairy			
	{Saanen	all white	high milk yield
	{British Saanen		
Swiss	{Toggenburg	brown/white	
	{Br. Toggenburg		
	{British Alpine	black/white	
	Anglo Nubian	any colour	high milk solids
	Golden Guernsey	chestnut/ginger	
	English	brown/black	
Fibre			
	Angora	usually white	produce mohair
	cashmere	any colour	produce cashmere
	Windsor White	white	
Meat			
	Boer	brown head/white body	
Others			
	Pygmy	any colour	
	Bagot	black head/shoulders, white body	

An eight-year-old castrated male with a female of similar age.

sourcing goats is one of the more difficult aspects. Basically, large numbers of mature goats do not come on to the market in the UK except when herds are closing and there is a dispersal sale, and furthermore, very few of these would be of correct and monitored health status for them to be exportable. Although quite a lot of goats are exported from the United Kingdom, most of these come from small pedigree herds. With this exception, adult goats are usually only offered for sale individually by breeders who have selected out surplus stock they do not want for their particular breeding programme. Sometimes these goats have faults, and it is important that those without experience should seek the help of someone who has, before they agree to buy. Goats are advertised in the monthly journal of the British Goat Society, in local free-ad papers, in local goat club magazines, and sometimes in farming and smallholding magazines.

Kids, on the other hand, are usually plentiful, as most goat keepers, large or small, produce more kids each year than they need for their own replacement programme. As it happens, kids mix together with very little trouble compared with adults, and as long as the cost of their upkeep without any financial return is not a problem, they are the preferred way to start up a goat herd. However, those intending to have just a few goats could quite possibly consider starting with adults and keeping them separate until they are more used to each other.

Note that when going to inspect goats for sale, the most sensible course of action is to take along someone with experience of goats, or at least livestock. There are many points of conformation and health that should be avoided, and these may not be apparent to an inexperienced person.

If the intention is to derive some income from the goats it is important to see some evidence of the productivity of the herd. With dairy goats this will be in the form of milk records, and records of success in recognized competitions. The British Goat Society has a system of awards for goats with a good milking performance, which to the novice may seem a little complicated. In short, in recognized milking competitions points are awarded for yield, butterfat and protein, and these are added together. A goat that gains 18 points is awarded a star (*), for 20 points a Q star (*). If the progeny of such goats also gain awards, they are given a numerical affix to denote the performance of their ancestors: thus a goat awarded the affix Q*3 will have had a dam, grand-dam and great grand-dam who will have qualified for either a star or Q star. An 'R' prefix denotes a goat that has produced more than 1,000kg (2,200lb) in an officially

Goats are easy to lead.

Mature males are strong, and during the breeding season can be very smelly.

recorded milk yield: for example, 'R150' indicates a recorded yield of 1,500kg (3,307lb).

Male goats are also awarded prefixes indicating the milk yield of their ancestors. A dagger prefix (†) indicates a male whose dam and sire's dam are both entitled to a star or Q star. A section mark (§) indicates a male whose dam is entitled to an R prefix: thus a male with the prefix R180/130 would indicate one whose dam has produced a lactation of 1,800kg (3,970lb) and the grand-dam 1,300kg (2,870lb). A male goat who has sired five daughters gaining a star, Q star or the prefix AR, RM or R, is given the prefix 'SM' (Sire of Merit).

More details of these and other awards are published in the British Goat Society's *Year Book*.

Fibre-producing goats are a little easier to judge as their product is carried on their back. Thus the quality of an Angora goat can be largely assessed by expert examination of its mohair (as long as they have not just been shorn).

HANDLING

Goats are naturally very friendly animals, and keepers should make the most of this trait. If they are well treated they are much easier to handle – and conversely, because they are quick in both mind and body, they can easily get the better of anyone trying to catch or hold them against their will.

Once they are used to being handled – which all hand-reared goats will be already – goats are easy to lead using a collar and lead. Most operations – such as foot trimming and giving injections – can be carried out with the goat tethered by means of a collar to the nearest fence or hurdle. Angora goats, because they have a broader back than dairy breeds and a thick fleece, can be cast onto their rumps in the same way as sheep.

All goats are very strong for their size, and it is therefore very important to handle them and lead them in such a way that they cannot escape or inadvertently hurt themselves or their keeper. Mature male goats need particularly careful handling as they are very strong, and for a large part of the year extremely smelly, which often causes people to handle them incorrectly. It is best to keep some old overalls specifically for handling males so that they can be grasped firmly without the worry of their smell being transferred to one's clothes.

Kids and young goats are best carried or transported in some form of covered trolley.

Horned goats can be more of a problem, particularly if others in a group are without horns. Most horned goats are much more bossy, and can sometimes be aggressive. For this reason goats that are to be handled frequently, such as the dairy breeds, should be disbudded as kids (*see* Chapter 9).

Kids are best transported in a box on a trolley or wheelbarrow.

A livestock trailer constructed on a car axle and capable of carrying three or four adult goats.

TRANSPORTING GOATS

Having decided on some goats, the new owner is faced with the problem of how to get them home. He need not worry unduly, however, as goats travel well in almost any vehicle: they are sure-footed, and as long as they are on a non-slip surface, cope quite well with normal vehicle movement.

The ideal floor is thick rubber matting as used in cow cubicles, covered with a thin layer of straw. A trailer or van can be used for adult goats. It is a legal require-ment that all vehicles used for animal transport should have a roof, and it is also important that there is nothing inside the vehicle which might cause injury. Land Rovers are not suitable because of the raised wheel arches, unless a flat floor is fitted; however, such a conversion would so much restrict the headroom that in a normal Land Rover there would only be room for young goats. Small kids can be carried in a large box or behind a dog-guard in an estate car or hatchback.

Whatever the vehicle, it is important that there is a partition between the driver and his load, otherwise it is quite possible that inquisitive goats will jump in and join him, thus creating a very dangerous situation. It is also important to remember that the interior of a closed van can get very hot, particularly in summer: good ventilation must therefore be provided, and regular stops are essential.

KEY POINTS

- Goats are inquisitive and agile, and can be difficult to contain.
- There are many breeds to choose from, producing milk, meat or fibre.
- When purchasing goats for the first time, take an experienced person with you.
- The friendliness of goats makes them rewarding pets.
- Male goats are large and smelly, and should not be kept unless suitable facilities are available.

2 Housing

The optimum housing environment for goats is very similar to that required by other livestock: it should provide plenty of air, plenty of light, enough room to be able to move around freely, good access to food and water, and a dry bed to lie on. Some goat keepers will no doubt be starting with existing buildings, others will be constructing something. Most farm-type buildings can be adapted for goats, as long as enough ventilation can be provided. Old, traditional livestock buildings tend to have thick walls, few windows or other openings, and low roofs, and with these it is important to enlarge any existing openings to allow a greater intake of air, and to make openings at the highest point in the roof – a ridge vent – to allow air out.

Another problem with many older buildings is that they are often impossible to clean out with machinery. Tractors are generally larger than they were years ago, and may not be able to get into buildings which in times past were serviced by smaller machines. This is a very import-ant consideration for anyone trying to make a living from their goats, where time inevitably means money. And by comparison with group pens, individual pens are more costly because they are even more time-consuming to clean out since the work must often be done by hand. However, goats are sociable animals once they have established a hierarchy, and seem to benefit from being housed together. Individual penning is used more

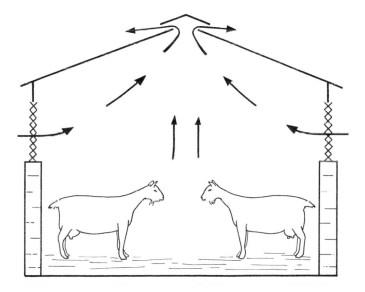

A well ventilated goat shed showing the movement of air out through an open ridge.

Unfamiliar goats housed together will often fight, and should be given more than average space until they have settled down.

by those with just a few goats, and by pedigree breeders who want to give individual attention to specific goats for show purposes.

The ideal building for goats is one with plenty of air space above them, and enough openings to allow good ventilation. For large numbers of goats the structure would have block walls to just above goat height, and then 'Yorkshire' boarding to the eaves. Normally the building would not need to be fully enclosed at each end, though if the prevailing weather were cold and wet, gates might need to be sheeted and the 'Yorkshire' boarding continued around the ends. A small number of goats could be kept in a garage-type building, but several openings would have to be made to enable air movement. A good way to allow air into a building without too much rain also blowing in is to cover openings with plastic 'windbreak' netting.

For goats housed in groups, a minimum of 1.75sq m (18.8sq ft) of floor space should be provided per goat. Owners of just a few goats may prefer to house them in individual pens, and these should be at least 1.5 by 2.5m (4.9 by 8.2ft).

Where goats are kept in groups it is important that there is enough trough or feed barrier space for them all to have access to their food; for this reason, group pens on commercial farms tend to be long and narrow.

HOUSING CONSTRUCTION

Although the optimum environment for goats is similar to that needed by most other farm livestock, the construction of any goat building needs special thought because they are so agile and inquisitive. Thus a shed that has housed cows or sheep for years without any problems may require a good deal of refurbishing before it is suitable for goats. Without the advantage of fingers, goats use their teeth and lips to investigate anything – meaning almost everything! – that interests them. To do this they will often stand up on their hindlegs, when they can reach up to at least 2m (6.5ft): if it is loose they will move it, if it is soft they will chew it, and so electric cables, switches, hosepipes, taps, door and

A 2cm (1in)-thick plank along a feed barrier that has been 'sculpted' by goats.

gate latches, putty, wood, paint and many other materials and fittings found in the average building are all fair game.

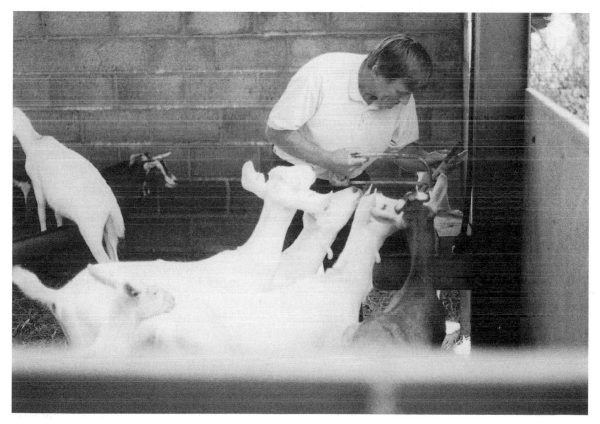

They use their lips and teeth to investigate all things that interest them!

They will jump onto window sills.

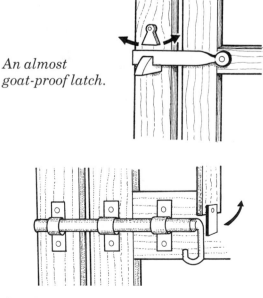

An almost goat-proof latch.

An almost goat-proof bolt.

Their agility also means they can jump up onto quite narrow ledges such as windowsills, which they will then use as a platform to reach things, or as a launching pad for jumping out. Fortunately it is usually only younger goats that are inclined to jump – older milkers rarely do this.

With careful consideration all these problems can be avoided, and indeed it is far easier to organize reconstruction at the outset, rather than with the goats in the building and all too ready to help with any modification work! Brick or block construction is most suitable, and as little timber as possible should be sited within reach of the goats. All water and electrical fittings should be well out of reach, and door and gate latches should be of a type that goats cannot undo. The latch and bolt

Trying to feed a group of goats inside their pen is always difficult.

Goats will usually climb into troughs which are inside their pen.

A self-filling drinking trough at a height which minimizes fouling of the water.

shown on p.30 can sometimes be opened if two goats play with them at the same time. One goat may flip up the swinging part as the other lifts the latch or slides the bolt – and hey presto! the gate or door is open!

Goats are very good at getting themselves caught on all manner of things, probably because they spend so much time fiddling with anything and everything – and gate or door bolts are favourites. For example, the bolt shown on p.30 has a hooked end, and there have been many instances of goats getting their mouth or cheek stuck as a result of chewing or licking them.

When constructing a shed for groups of goats, careful consideration should be given to the type of floor used. In straw-bedded pens there are two options: a self-draining, porous floor made from something like rolled stone chippings; or a solid floor such as concrete. A porous floor does not get so wet and is cheaper, but a solid floor allows a better standard of cleaning, and this may be important if there are ever health problems with the goats. Although well rolled stone can be surprisingly durable, a concrete floor will withstand the wear and tear of cleaning out with machinery such as a tractor or loader.

One of the most important things to consider when designing or constructing goat pens is ease of access, for getting goats in and out, for feeding and for cleaning out.

FEEDING SYSTEMS

Those people with just a few goats will probably be content with hayracks inside the pens, and buckets or troughs for concentrate or corn feed hanging inside or outside the pens; these should be placed in such a way that the goats can feed from them without fouling them too much. Note that haynets designed for horses are not suitable for goats – quite apart from the problem of their chewing the net material, there is a real chance that they will get caught up in them, and there have been cases of kids breaking their legs when playing 'king of the castle' on haynets.

Anyone who has ever gone into a pen of goats with a bucket or bag of food will appreciate the general preference for dispensing feed outside the pen, using any system where goats put their heads through one side of their pen in order to reach their food that is placed along the outside.

A supply of clean water should always be available. Water buckets should always be sited outside the pen, as this will prevent fouling of the water, although for groups of goats, self-filling water troughs will almost certainly be used. These will normally be sited in the pen, but in a position where they will not be too vulnerable to damage by machinery. To minimize the risk of the water becoming fouled by the goats, it is best to have the top of the trough at least 80cm (30in) from the floor, and to provide a few concrete blocks for the smaller goats to stand on so they can reach the water. Water pipes or fittings should be sited well out of reach, or be of such a design that they can withstand the investigative teeth and lips of inquisitive goats. The same applies to electrical equipment and fittings.

Pens for groups of goats are usually constructed so that one side comprises a feed barrier, designed so that the goats can put their heads out to reach their food,

A feed barrier with vertical bars and an adjustable iron rail to prevent smaller goats escaping.

A feed barrier with diagonal bars which helps reduce wastage of forage.

placed on its outside, such as hay and silage. With larger numbers of goats the building may be constructed with a passage running down the middle of two rows of pens, so that twice as many pens can be serviced from the one passage.

There are several designs for feed barriers, all intended to minimize the wastage of long forage such as hay. Basically they are made so it is difficult for the goats to bring their heads back through the barrier bars; some forages – such as maize silage – are harder to pull back through feed barriers than others. Note that long horizontal spaces are not suitable if groups are to be fed any form of concentrate, because during the struggle to get to the food, the goat on the end of the row might end up with its neck squashed against the vertical bars, by the sheer weight of the other goats pushing to get to the food. Young goats, who are always enthusiastic about everything, are a particular problem, and fatalities have occurred with this type of barrier.

SHELTER

It is most important that goats kept outside can keep dry, so they will need access to shelter. Very often a three-sided shelter will be sufficient, especially if it can be sited in a sheltered part of the field or paddock. Bear in mind that meat and fibre goats will be kept out on grass much more than dairy goats, and field shelters in particular for fibre animals such as Angoras often have slatted floors to prevent their fleece from becoming soiled or contaminated with bedding material.

As shelters tend to be used most when it is wet, the area around them is likely to become very muddy, in which case it is helpful to be able to move them to a clean spot. Skids under the base and a towing point will therefore prove to be a great advantage.

Field shelters are not usually very high, and it is important that they are strongly constructed because the goats will often

34

An electrified 'hot wire' on the inside of a square-mesh stock fence.

A 'hot wire' along the top of a stock fence to stop goats reaching over.

A 'hot wire' helping to protect a young apple tree.

jump onto the roof during enthusiastic games of 'king of the castle' – and collapsed shelters are at the least a nuisance, and at worst can be dangerous for the goats underneath.

Several small shelters, or ones that are partitioned, may be an advantage, as one bossy goat can easily prevent other goats from sheltering. It is quite common to see the lowest-ranking goats being forced to seek shelter against the outside during bad weather.

FENCING

There is no such thing as a 100 per cent goat-proof fence. Some systems will stay good for quite a while; some will last for only a few minutes. Goats love to stand up against fences resting their front feet on the rails or mesh, and if this is done in the same place over and over again – usually to reach an overhanging shrub or tree – even the strongest fence will collapse in time. This habit can be effectively curtailed by running an electric 'hot wire' around the fence, (9–12in (20–30cm) out from the fence, and 9–12in (20–30cm) from the ground).

Wire-mesh fences do not last very long because of the clambering activity just described, and if electric fencing cannot be used, a strong horizontal rail placed along the top of the fence may save damage to the mesh by giving the goats somewhere to rest their feet.

If electric fencing is to be used rather than wire mesh, then semi-permanent fencing using tensioned plain wire is preferable; if erected well in the first place, and maintained regularly, this should remain goat-proof for long periods. Five wires are necessary, even though it may be possible to leave the bottom wire disconnected in some situations. It is most important that the fence is working well

A five-wire, tensioned, semi-permanent electrified fence.

36

at all times, because goats learn quickly if the power has dropped or, worse still, has failed completely, and they may well then clamber through the fence.

Electrified plastic mesh is not so good for goats for two reasons: first, they will graze right up to, and sometimes under an electric fence, which is probably why they learn so quickly that it is not working. And in this case, if they graze close to electrified mesh, there is a chance that, should they touch it and receive a shock, they may jerk back and in doing so catch an ear tag or horn in the mesh. There have been cases of goats and sheep becoming fatally entangled in this type of fencing.

The other problem is that goats often learn quite quickly that the horizontal wires do not carry any current, and they may then choose to chew through these wires thus causing a lot of expensive damage. Barbed wire is not recomm-ended, as the goats' clambering habits will sooner or later almost certainly result in injury.

TETHERING

For those with just one or two pet goats, tethering is a reasonable option. It is not an ideal way of constraining animals, but it does mean that they can be outside, and it avoids the problems of trying to erect goat-proof fencing. However, it is most important to remember that goats on tethers are vulnerable: for instance, they may be bothered by children or dogs, and for this reason alone they must be regularly checked. Ideally they should be within sight of someone who will look out for signs of trouble.

The goat's inquisitive and active nature has already been described, and this can also create problems. Thus a tether must be sited where there is no chance of the animal becoming entangled, which means it should be away from bushes and trees. Furthermore, if the goat has access to shelter, unless this is constructed very carefully there will always be a risk of the tether becoming caught up. Nevertheless if, after all this, a tether seems to be the best way of constraining a goat, then it should be made from light, strong chain, and there should be swivels at each end and in the middle.

KEY POINTS

- With larger numbers of goats it is important that the sheds have tractor access.
- Good ventilation is very important.
- Take care that 'goat-proof' door and gate latches are fitted.
- Goats can be wasteful feeders, and feeding systems need to minimize this.
- It is preferable to be able to feed groups of goats without entering their pen.
- Goats kept outside need shelter from the rain.
- An electrified 'hot wire' will usually prevent goats clambering through or over mesh stock fencing.
- Tethering one or two goats avoids the need for fencing, but much care must be given to the design and situation.

A tether using a chain with a swivel at each end and in the middle.

3 Nutrition and Feeding

Many aspects of the nutrition and feeding of goats are similar to other farmed species. It is a ruminant like the sheep and the cow, and anyone used to these will understand the principles involved as regards optimizing nutrition in order to achieve the best possible performance. The goat is potentially a very productive animal, and if compared weight for weight, a dairy goat will produce significantly more milk than the equivalent dairy cow. However, it can only do this if it is fed properly, and this means a daily intake of an adequate quantity of feed of the correct nutrional value, and in a form that it will eat.

THE RUMINANT SYSTEM

The most striking feature of ruminants is their complicated stomach sytem that enables them to digest large quantities of plant material. All ruminants take in large quantities of plant material

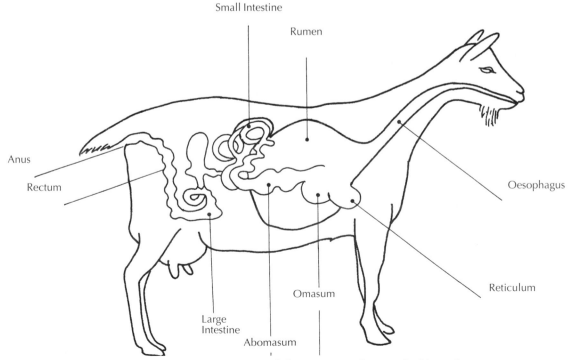

A diagram showing the relative position of the organs of a goat's digestive tract.

relatively quickly, which they will regurgitate and chew again later, during a quiet period of the day or night; they will then swallow it back into the digestive system. This action of chewing food for the second time is called 'cudding' or 'chewing the cud' and is presumed to be something that has evolved to allow this group of herbivores to harvest their food quickly, because this is when they are most vulnerable to preditors, and to chew it properly later when they have settled themselves in a position of greater safety.

The main organ of a ruminant's gut is the rumen or first stomach. This is a very large organ which contains a diverse population of micro-organisms that secrete enzymes which will break down the cellulose of the plant cell walls and make the nutrients therein available. The population of micro-organisms in the rumen will vary according to the material being eaten, and for this reason sudden changes in the feed may be harmful to goats. This will be discussed later in the chapter on health. Feed material remains in the rumen until it has been broken down into a form that will allow it to pass on down through the rest of the digestive system.

In young ruminants the rumen does not begin to function until they are 2–3 weeks old, and the milk they drink bypasses the rumen via a structure called the oesophageal groove, and goes straight into the last stomach or abomasum. The abomasum is equivalent to the single stomach of non-ruminants. Sometimes when young, artificially reared kids drink too quickly the milk does flow into the rumen, and if this happens there is a risk that the kids will become bloated due to an excess of gas building up there.

Digestion

The rumen microbes break down the starch, protein and fibre in the feed, and volatile fatty acids (VFAs) are released, along with the gas methane. The VFAs are absorbed through the rumen wall and are the animal's main source of energy. The proportions of the different VFAs will vary according to the feed. Acetic and proprionic acid are produced in greatest quantities, but with a little butyric acid.

The methane is removed by belching (eructation), but sometimes this is prevented by obstructions or torsion in the gut, which will result in the goat becoming bloated. Sometimes the obstruction can be froth that has been produced by fermentation of the feed; if this is the case, medicants can be given to disperse it. When fibre is fermented, large amounts of acetic acid will be produced, whereas the starch and sugars from cereal-based concentrate feeds will produce large amounts of proprionic acid.

The varying amounts and the degree of absorption of the different VFAs will affect the composition of the milk. Acetic acid is used for synthesizing milk fat, whereas milk yield is governed by lactose production from glucose, which is itself synthesized from proprionic acid. Thus the feeds offered to goats can have a marked effect on the compositional quality of the milk, and this will be most important to those processing milk into other dairy products.

Some of the protein in the feed will be used (degraded) by the rumen microbes to make their own microbial protein, and some of this will be an important source of nutrients for the ruminant animal, in this case the goat.

Urea can be fed as a source of non-protein nitrogen which will be utilized by the rumen microbes, along with any urea recycled from the protein in the feed. When urea is broken down in the rumen, ammonia is formed, and excessive levels of this in the blood can be toxic.

Once food has reached the abomasum, the digestive process is similar to that in monogastric animals. Nutrients are absorbed in the abomasum, and in the large and small intestines. The food material, however, having passed through the rumen system, will be quite different to that in monogastric animals: most of the protein will be microbial protein, the fibre will be largely indigestible, and most of the starch and sugar will have been utilized by the rumen.

NUTRIENT REQUIREMENTS

All animals need a specific minimum intake of nutrients to be able to function; the amount required will vary according to the level of work their body is required to do. The lowest requirement will be for animals that are neither growing, reproducing or lactating – in other words, they are just maintaining their bodies at a normal, non-productive level: this level of requirement is normally called 'maintenance'. The other level is known as 'production', which may be subdivided into 'pregnancy', 'lactation', and 'growth'.

Another factor that has a major influence on an animal's intake of nutrients will be its appetite. Animals can only eat a certain amount of food each day, and this appetite for food is usually described as the 'dry matter intake' or 'DMI'. It is important to quantify appetite in terms of dry matter, as this is the part of the food that contains the nutrients; furthermore, dry matter is always constant, whereas the fresh weight of a given material will be dictated by its water content and therefore extremely variable. For example, a daily appetite or food intake of 2.5kg (5.5lb) of turnips would be very different to an intake of 2.5kg of barley.

The dry matter intake will vary according to the weight of the animal, and in the case of goats this will be

approximately 3.5 per cent of its bodyweight per day. It is possible to increase this, and because goats are inquisitive feeders this can often be achieved by giving them something different at intervals throughout the day. This would not be practicable for a larger scale commercial farmer, although turning the hay or pushing forward the silage in feed passages at intervals during the day will often encourage goats to feed, even when they are apparently content and are lying down cudding.

Having established that the amount of food a goat is capable of eating is limited, the next stage is to consider how much energy and protein it will require for maintainance, growth or production. Once this has been calculated, it is then possible to devise a suitable ration that should satisfy these requirements.

Energy

The unit of energy used in animal feeding tables is the joule, or more precisely the megajoule (MJ). In most feed tables energy will be expressed as 'metabolizable energy', so a goat will require a minimum number of megajoules (MJ) to satisfy its requirement for metabolizable energy (ME), and this will vary according to its physiological and productive state at the time. The energy requirements for goats at the three levels of production may be expressed thus:

Maintenance: $0.5MJME/kg^{0.75}$ of metabolic bodyweight (liveweight in kg to the power of 0.75);
Pregnancy: $0.5MJME/kg^{0.75}$ rising to $0.7MJME/kg^{0.75}$ for the last month;
Lactation: maintenance needs + 5MJME per kg milk produced (3.5% butter fat).

Anyone familiar with the requirements for cattle will realize that the above requirements are very similar to those for dairy cows.

Various other factors – such as air temperature, the fat content of the milk, and exercise – will affect a goat's energy requirements. For example, if it is out in a grazing field or paddock it will need more energy than one that is housed, and therefore an extra 1.5–2.5MJ should be allowed for goats that are outside.

Less is known about the requirements of fibre-producing goats, though evidence suggests that the Angora goat will produce mohair at the expense of other body functions when nutrition is limited. For example, a high incidence of abortion has been reported for Angoras in harsh environments in South Africa and the USA, and it is now understood that this was due to inadequate energy intakes.

Protein

As the protein requirements, and protein degradation, in ruminant animals become better understood, some will suggest that recommendations for the amounts of protein required at the various levels of growth and production become more

complicated. In the latest literature these are given in terms of 'totally absorbed amino-acid nitrogen'. The recommendations for maintainance in goats are in the range 0.35–0.41g AA-N/kg$^{0.75}$, and for lactation an additional 6.9g of AA-N will be required for each kg of milk.

Those who studied more than twenty-five years ago may be more familiar with protein requirements being given as grammes of digestible crude protein (DCP). The protein from different feed materials will be broken down or degraded by the rumen micro organisms in different amounts, and that which is undegraded will go on through the gut to be absorbed and thus used by the animal. Some tables of requirements will give figures for DCP, rumen degraded protein (RDP) and undegraded dietary protein (UDP). As a guide, approximately 9g of RDP should be supplied per MJME. While DCP does not give the full picture, it is a useful guide to feeding at the practical level, and anyone using these older systems will find they are able to devise correct rations for their goats. The table below gives the dry matter appetite, energy and protein (DCP) requirements for lactating and growing goats:

The Nutrient Requirements for Goats of Different Weights and with Different Milk Yields

liveweight (kg)	milk yield (kg/day3.5%BF)	dry matter appetite (kg/day)	ME (MJ/day)	DCP (g/day)
	0	1.5	8.0	51
	1	1.7	13.1	90
50	2	1.9	18.2	147
	3	2.1	23.3	195
	4	2.3	28.4	243
	0	2.1	10.3	66
	1	2.3	15.4	114
70	2	2.5	20.5	162
	3	2.7	25.6	210
	4	2.9	30.7	258
	5	3.1	35.8	306
	6	3.3	41.1	354

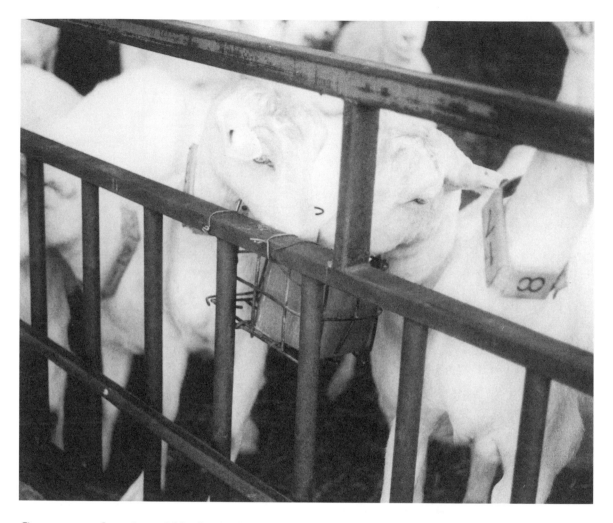

Goats around a mineral block in a 'cage' to prevent it being destroyed too quickly.

Mineral and Trace Element Requirements for Lactating Goats

milk yield (kg)	Ca (g/d)	P (g/d)	NaCl (g/d)	K (g/d)	Cu (mg/kg) DM	Zn (mg/kg) DM	Co (mg/kg) DM	I (mg/kg) DM	Mn (mg/kg) DM	Fe (mg/kg) Dm	Se (mg/kg) DM
1	4.5	4.8	11.5	3.3	}						
2	7.3	7.8	13.0	5.4	}						
3	10.2	10.9	14.5	7.5	}10-20	50-80	< 10	8-20	40-60	30-40	<3
4	13.0	14.0	16.0	9.6	}						
5	15.9	17.1	17.5	11.7	}						

Protein is required for the growth of new tissue in the growing animal or in the case of injury. It is also required for milk and hair production. High-yielding goats and fast-growing kids may not get an adequate supply of amino-acids from microbial protein, and so it will be necessary to provide extra, undegradable protein (UDP) as part of their daily ration.

Minerals and Trace Elements

With their comparatively small body as compared with their high levels of production, it is reasonable to expect the problems of mineral imbalance as so often seen in high-yielding cows, such as hypercalcaemia and hypomagnasaemia. In reality problems of mineral deficiency or toxicity are rare in goats, and it is likely that the selective feeding behaviour of the goat allows it to choose feed materials containing the minerals it requires. Most concentrate feeds contain a mineral and trace element supplement, and these plus mineral blocks in their pens should ensure that the goats will not have any problems in this area.

Although there are gaps in our knowledge, there has been some scientific work on this aspect of goat nutrition, and this, plus what is already known about other ruminants, makes it possible to compile a list of recommended levels for mineral and trace element requirements.

Less is known about the requirements of fibre-producing goats, and until more information is available it would be prudent to use the recommendations for sheep. There is some evidence to suggest that Angora goats, for example, may have similar requirements to sheep for copper, and thus it would be possible to induce copper toxicity if too much were given in

Adventurous goats browsing a tree in Morocco.

A simple hayrack made by bending a piece of weldmesh into a cylinder.

the diet, especially if they were grazing in a copper-rich environment.

Water

Depending on a number of factors, a goat may drink up to 18 litres (4gals) of water a day. Climatic conditions, type of feed and state of lacatation will all influence water intake. A lactating goat requires 1.43 litres (0.3gals) of water per 1kg (2.2lb) of milk produced, and will not milk well if the availability of water is limited.

Goats are quite fussy about the water they drink, and will not drink as much as they should if the water is dirty – although being goats, there will always be some who seem to prefer stale water to fresh! Some goat keepers offer warm water to encourage their high-yielding goats to drink; however, it is doubtful if this can be justified on economic grounds, as the

Goats like maize silage because they can pick out many different parts of the plant.

increase in milk yield is unlikely to offset the cost of heating the water.

FEED MATERIALS

In common with other ruminants, goats have a digestive system that has developed to cope with large quantities of plant material which, compared with some other foods such as meat, is of relatively low nutritional value. If it has the opportunity, the domesticated goat, like its wild ancestors, will spend a lot of time ranging around looking for those plant species it prefers. It is well known that goats are browsers rather than grazers, and they will spend much more time eating leaves and bark from trees and shrubs than they will eating grass.

Goats have been wrongly accused of creating several of the world's deserts because of their browsing tendencies, which many consider destructive. The reality is that they are often the only animals that can survive in an environment that has been overgrazed by

---

Some Common Poisonous Plants

Acorns (unripe)	Daffodil	Potato (raw)
Anemone	Deadly nightshade	Privet
Bindweed	Dog's mercury	Prunus leaves (when dry)
Black nightshade	Foxglove	Ragwort
Box	Henbane	Rhodedendron
Bracken	Kale	Rhubarb leaves
Bryony	Laburnum	Snowdrop
Buttercup	Laurel	Spindle
Celandine	Narcissus	Yew
Charlock (seeds)	Potato (haulm)	

---

cattle and sheep, and in this situation they eat all that is left: the trees. However, if properly managed, goats can contribute a lot in terms of food production in environments that cannot support sheep or cattle.

Most people who keep just a few goats will allow them to graze in small paddocks, and in this situation they will graze quite effectively if there is nothing else to browse. One hectare of grazing (2.5 acres) will support five to seven goats, depending on the quality of the forage that is grown. Larger commercial units, almost without exception, will house their goats all the time and will feed conserved forage materials such as maize, grass or lucerne silage or hay; they may also cut and carry green forage when it is plentiful.

If offered forage that they really like, such as lucerne, goats will eat approximately 100g/kg metabolic body-weight (liveweight $^{0.75}$). They will also readily consume rye grass and vetches, though they do not seem to like growing white clover. Goats have a natural preference for material with a high dry-matter content: thus they seem to prefer maize or lucerne silage to grass silage. Often they will only eat certain plants when these have wilted, but not when they are fresh; this is particularly true of stinging nettles, so if goats are required to

tidy up areas of rough grazing, it helps if the nettles are knocked down first.

When feeding conserved forage, particularly any form of hay, it must be noted that goats can be very wasteful feeders. In their efforts to select the parts of the forage they like most, they will pull a lot out from a hayrack – and once this has been trodden on and fouled, they will not eat it. Hayracks and feeders that restrict the amount that can be pulled out are therefore an advantage.

Most smaller-scale goat keepers will offer hay to their goats as their main source of forage. In general goats prefer late-cut seed hay rather than soft meadow hay; they have a natural preference for stemmy material, and will eat nettles, docks and many other plants that may be in the hay. Grass that contains a variety of plants such as docks, clover and vetches will make good hay for goats.

Most of the larger goat farms will feed maize silage as the main source of forage if they are in an area where maize can be grown, and this is a very good feed for goats: it is nutritious, it has many different parts so the goats can spend a lot of time picking out the preferred parts first, and it is relatively dry. Grass silage tends to be more variable, particularly in water content, and this can affect intake by as much as fifty per cent.

Note that silage can be a source of the disease listeriosis. Maize silage is less of a risk than grass silage – particularly if the latter is in bags – because the causal bacteria cannot thrive at a low pH. Cases of listeriosis do occur, however, amongst goats fed maize silage; it is assumed that the bacteria survive in parts of the silage that have not been made so well, such as around the edges of the clamp or where there are air pockets.

Goats will eat a very wide range of plant materials, besides a number of by-product materials that would not be considered nutritious enough for dairy cows, such as pea and bean haulm, all types of straw, and fruit pulp. These usually have a high dry matter content, and as long as they can be offered in large quantities, so that the goats can be selective, a high level of performance can often be achieved for a relatively low cost.

The hobby goat keeper will consider kitchen scraps for her stock, but in this she should step carefully: for instance, brassicas such as cabbage, kale and rape may interfere with iodine absorption, and large quantities of kale can cause anaemia. As a precaution, these materials should not make up more than 30 per cent of the diet of lactating goats. Carrots, swedes and other root crops will be enjoyed, although goats will be less keen to eat those that have been freshly dug with soil still around them. And when feeding any kitchen or garden waste it must be remembered that there are many plants, or parts of plants, that will be poisonous.

If grazing outside, goats are generally quite good at not poisoning themselves, and are less likely to do so than cows or sheep; however, it is better to deny them access to plants that are known to be harmful.

Forage material alone will not provide enough nutrients for goats at times of high demand such as during late pregnancy and most of the lactation period. It is normal at these times to feed material of higher nutritional value, or where the nutrients are more concentrated, and these concentrate feeds are usually made up by a feed mill. For sheep and cattle there is always a large range to choose from, and most manufacturers will do at least one goat mix. These feeds are usually made up from a mixture of ingredients to give a guaranteed analysis of protein, fibre and energy. The ingredients used may include barley, wheat, oats, maize, peas and beans, and meals such as those from soya, rape and linseed. Many of these will be heated during processing, and this can protect some of the protein from rumen degradation. Fishmeal is another good source of undegraded protein, though it may not be enjoyed so much by goats when incorporated in their feed.

Most animal feed manufacturers will make their various concentrate feeds to a fixed analysis, but the formula, or list of ingredients, will change according to what is cheapest at the time of mixing. This has caused problems for some commercial goat farms, where several tonnes of pelleted or cubed feed have been ordered and delivered, only for the mix to be rejected by the goats because apparently they did not like one particular ingredient, with a concomitant drop in milk production.

A lot of goat keepers favour coarse mixes, where the ingredients are not pelleted or cubed, but are left in their natural form as a loose mix. For the larger scale farmer these mixes are usually considered too expensive as compared with a pelleted or cubed feed, especially as the goats are able to select the ingredients they like best, and will sometimes reject parts of the mix. This is wasteful and expensive, and of course will mean the goats are not getting the correct balance of nutrients. At the hobby level, however, it is nice to see what is in the feed, and the extra cost is not so significant when only buying a few bags at a time.

Some Typical Nutritive Values for some Forages and Root Crops

	Dry matter (%)	ME (MJ/kg DM)	Crude protein (g/kgDM)	RDP (g/kgDM)	UDP (g/kgDM)	Crude fibre (g/kgDM)
Silage						
Grass (good quality)	27	10.2	170	136	34	300
Lucerne	25	8.5	168	101	67	256
Maize	21	10.8	110	66	44	233
Hay						
Grass	85	9	101	81	20	320
Lucerne (half flower)	85	8.2	225	180	45	302
Red clover	85	8.9	161	129	32	287
Straw						
Spring barley	86	7.3	38	30	8	394
Spring oats	86	6.7	34	27	7	394
Winter wheat	86	5.7	24	10	5	426
Roots						
Turnips	9	11.2	70	98	24	111
Swedes	10	12.8	64	86	22	100
Fodder beet	18	12.5	50	-	-	53
Green crops						
Grass (monthly cut)	20	11.2	175	105	70	225
Lucerne (in bud)	22	9.4	205	123	82	282
Cabbage	11	10.4	136	82	54	182
Kale	16	11.1	137	82	55	200

Nutritive Values of some Grains and Legume Seeds

	Dry matter (%)	ME (MJ/kg DM)	Crude protein (g/kgDM)	RDP (g/kgDM)	UDP (g/kgDM)	Crude fibre (g/kgDM)
Barley	86	13.7	108	86	22	53
Oats	86	11.5	109	87	22	121
Wheat	86	14.0	124	99	25	26
Maize	86	14.2	98	59	39	24
Field beans	86	12.8	290	232	58	85
Peas	86	13.4	262	157	105	64
Soya meal	90	12.3	503	302	201	58

Nutritive Values for some By-Products

	Dry matter (%)	ME (MJ/kg DM)	Crude protein (g/kgDM)	RDP (g/kgDM)	UDP (g/kgDM)	Crude fibre (g/kgDM)
Dried brewer's grain	90	10.3	204	122	82	169
Sugar beet pulp (dried & molasses	90	12.2	106	64	42	144
Maize gluten	90	14.2	394	315	79	23
Wheat middlings	88	11.9	176	141	35	86
Wheat bran	88	10.1	170	136	34	114
Linseed cake	90	13.4	332	199	133	102

Virtually all concentrate feeds have a high proportion of cereal grains: in pelleted feeds this is likely to be barley; in loose mixes there may be a high proportion of oats. Note, however, that if goats are offered too much of these cereal-based feeds, various problems can occur – as a general rule, no more than 40 per cent of the total feed intake should consist of concentrates.

A lot of research has been carried out, particularly with sheep, showing that it is preferable to feed cereal grains whole rather than rolled or broken as they are in most feeds. Whole grain is retained in the digestive system longer, and is utilized more effectively, whereas rolled or broken grains, by comparison, create more acid conditions in the digestive tract. This will have a harmful effect on the gut wall, which in turn will adversely effect the digestive processes. The problem with feeding whole grains to goats is that they will often pick them out and leave other essential parts of the feed, such as the meals that are included to raise the level of protein. If a mix based on whole grains can be formulated, that the goats will eat up completely, this will be the healthiest and cheapest way of feeding concentrates.

THE NUTRITIVE VALUE OF FEEDSTUFFS

In the previous section various feed materials were discussed, and a number of factors will be considered in deciding which to incorporate in a goat's daily ration of feed. The most important question is, will the goats eat it? Although they will eat a greater variety of plant species than either cows or sheep, they are still quite fussy animals and will reject any material they consider unpalatable or spoiled. Their manipulative mouths give them the ability to avoid the smallest of particles, and it is virtually impossible to disguise anything in their feed.

Having decided or discovered what the goats will eat, the next question is, how much? We have seen that concentrate feeds are offered because the goat is just not capable of eating enough forage material at times of high demand, to satisfy its requirements for nutrients. Thus, to be able to consider any material for incorporation into a goat's daily ration, the feed value of each must be considered.

NUTRITIONAL VALUE: TERMS EXPLAINED

Dry Matter

When assessing both the nutritive and monetary value of feed materials it is important to know the dry matter content: this is usually expressed as a percentage. From the tables above it can be seen that the amount of metabolizable energy in a root crop such as turnips is similar to that in oats. However, because of the low dry matter content of turnips it would be necessary for the goats to eat 9kg (20lb) to obtain the same amount of energy as in 1kg (2.2lb) of oats.

The important points from this calculation are that the goats would not be able to eat 9kg of turnips in a day, and one would have to pay very much less for the turnips if one was looking for value for money. Other factors such as transport, ease of handling and storage will be of particular concern to the goat farmer who will be dealing with several tonnes of feed material at one time.

Digestibility

This is usually expressed as the 'D'-value, or as 'digestible organic matter' (DOMD). This is the percentage of organic or non-mineral matter in the dry feed material that is digested by the animal. The values may range from 40–90 per cent.

Metabolizable Energy (ME)

This the amount of energy in a feed material that is available to the animal after the feed has been digested. The unit of ME is the megajoule (MJ or 1 million joules). Some readers may be more familiar with the calorie as a unit of energy: one calorie is equal to 4.184 joules.

Digestible Crude Protein

In the scientific world DCP is no longer used as a measure of protein in animal feeds. However, at the practical feeding level it is still a useful measure, and will still be found on many of the analysis statements from feed manufacturers.

It is now known that the efficiency of protein utilization is influenced by the level of protein degradation in the rumen, and if a large amount is degraded in the rumen, this leaves only a small amount available to the animal.

In modern tables some indication of the rumen degradability (RDP) and the amount undegraded (UDP) will be given. Nevertheless, all of these values can only be used as a guide, as many factors will affect the value of any sample of feed material. The only accurate way of formulating a feed mix to obtain a specific level of nutrients would be to have each batch of ingredients analysed.

MAKING UP RATIONS FOR GOATS

Several factors will influence the choice of feedstuffs used to make up a daily ration for goats – and whichever feed materials are used, a goat should always be offered both forage and concentrates.

A goat farmer will be looking for a combination of feedstuffs that will ensure that his/her goats give the best performance for the least cost. The pet goat keeper will be more interested in convenience and the goat's state of health, and within reason, cost will not be so important.

There will also be circumstances when the main purpose of giving goats concentrate feeds will be to keep them tame and friendly, and not particularly for their nutrient requirement.

When formulating rations it is useful to have some idea of the goats' bodyweight: from this, and from information about their performance, it is possible to calculate their requirements for nutrients. It is then a question of considering what feeds are available. Most smaller-scale goat keepers will use hay as the main conserved forage, and will supplement this with vegetables and vegetable waste. The concentrate feed may be home-mixed or a made-up mixture, or 'nuts' bought from the local feed merchant, and it will be offered in appropriate quantities to give the level of nutrients required.

A good starting point for the novice goat keeper is hay as the main source of forage, plus ready-made concentrates. As experience is gained, it will be possible to add other feedstuffs to the goats' daily ration – but always with careful consideration as to the nutritional value of these. Many people with just a small number of goats will no doubt keep them outside in a small field or paddock, where they will graze grass and many other plant species; during the spring and summer they could get all their forage in this way.

To assess if the goats are getting enough nutrients in this situation, make a rough calculation of their dry matter intake, and then, using published tables, calculate the value of the grass and other roughage that they are likely to eat in one day. As with conserved forages, at times of high performance such as mid-lactation it is unlikely the goats will be able to satisfy their needs from fresh forage alone.

In general, most pet goats – like other pet animals – tend to be over-fed. A fat goat is usually an unhealthy goat, and so this scenario should be avoided. Very few health problems are the consequence of goats being a little underweight, as compared with those brought about by obesity.

KEY POINTS

- Goats are ruminants like sheep and cows, and feeding them follows the same principles.
- Dairy goats' requirements for nutrients are almost identical to those for dairy cows.
- There are published tables to help calculate a goat's requirements for nutrients at different stages and levels of production.
- A goat will eat a wide range of feed materials but will be fussy about any that are spoiled.
- It is important to know what plants are poisonous if feeding garden waste.
- Once a goat's nutrient requirements have been assessed, the best plan is to refer to published tables that give the nutritional value of most feed materials: these will help you formulate a ration for your goat.
- Pet goats tend to be overfed, and their health can be jeopardized by their being too fat.

A goat that is too fat, on the right, compared with one in good condition.

4 Breeding and Reproduction

Probably the most interesting aspect of keeping a productive animal such as the goat is to breed from it. Kidding time is always exciting, as one can never be sure how things will turn out, what problems will arise, and what sort of kids will be produced; for instance, if the goats are of mixed breeds it is always interesting to see what markings or colour patterns are produced. Most goat keepers will be interested in improving their goats, however many they keep, and will hope that each new generation will be an improvement over the one before.

In general, all aspects of reproduction in the goat are similar to sheep. They have more or less the same reproduction cycle, and their anatomy is practically the same. Thus anyone used to breeding sheep should be able to cope with breeding goats – which means the novice goat keeper should cultivate a friendship with the local sheep farmer, particularly during the first kidding season!

THE BREEDING SEASON

Most people think of the breeding season as the time of the year when goats mate. Goats in countries away from the Equator are influenced by the varying lengths of night and day according to the season, and are only receptive to the male at specific times of the year. In the northern hemisphere this will be in the autumn, and in Great Britain usually some time during September or October.

Once the breeding season begins, the female goats will regularly go through periods of receptivity to the male, usually called the 'oestrus' or 'heat period'. At this time they show marked changes in behaviour, which thankfully make it obvious as to when they are ready to go to the male (unlike in the cow). The most obvious sign of oestrus is tail wagging. The goat will stand near the male, if she can, or near another receptive goat, and rapidly wag her tail sideways. She will probably be very vocal at this time, and these two signs together are characteristic of heat, or oestrus. Other signs are more subtle, and may include loss of appetite, a raised temperature and a drop in milk yield. If a goat is kept on her own, the signs of oestrus are not always so obvious – but even in this situation one would expect her to be looking anxiously out of her pen, crying and wagging her tail.

Females who are not showing clear signs of oestrus may be 'teased': a trick used by many experienced goat keepers is to keep a rag impregnated with the smell of a male goat in a sealed jar, and to bring this out for any such female to smell. It is said that such a 'billy-rag' will often induce oestrous behaviour in a goat that may otherwise show no signs at all.

Goats with tropical origins tend to have a longer breeding season. Anglo-Nubians and Pygmy goats tend to come into first oestrus earlier than other breeds, and if unmated will often continue to cycle well into March.

Breeding Cycle
Duration of the breeding season   Sept–Feb*
Onset of oestrus   Sept–Oct
Duration of oestrus cycle   21 days
Ovulation   24–36 hours after onset of oestrus
Gestation period   150 +/–1 days
Number of kids   1–5
Age sexually mature   3–6 months
* Depends on breed

MATING

It is hard to justify keeping a male goat if you have only a few females. As already discussed, male goats are strong and smelly, and not everyone will be able to provide the necessary level of care to keep them safely and without trouble. Also, those with only a few goats will quickly run into problems with inbreeding – when a male mates with his own daughters or even granddaughters. Unless one has several males this can be difficult to avoid, and if it does happen it can result in undesirable characteristics appearing in the progeny. Thus the person who keeps just a few goats will probably have to find the nearest suitable male, or consider the use of artificial insemination (AI).

Most goat keepers will be interested in breeding for improvement, and will therefore want to use a selected male of known pedigree. The best way to discover where to find suitable males is as a member of the British Goat Society or one of the local goat societies or clubs affiliated to the British Goat Society or the British Angora Goat Society.

Once a suitable male has been identified, it is then a question of getting the female to him, and at the right time in her oestrous cycle. As the goat keeper gains experience it becomes easier to judge the best time; a

general rule is not to go too soon. If the female is only just showing signs of oestrus in the morning, it is better to wait until the afternoon. Unfortunately, although goats travel well, the trauma of the journey can upset them so that on arrival they will not stand for the male. This is more of a problem with young, inexperienced goats.

Dairy males will usually be very keen to mount a female, even if she is unwilling. Some other breeds, such as Angoras, are more reticent, and may not mount the female if too many unfamiliar people are around at the time. If a male spends a lot of time sniffing and displaying without mounting the female it is usually a sign that she is not properly on heat, or that he is not feeling well – or maybe that he is getting too old. At best the male will mount the female quickly; when ejaculation takes place, he will jerk his head back. Sometimes a male will mount again, although one good mating is all that is necessary.

Mature males have some unpleasant habits, particularly during the breeding season!

Dairy males are usually keen to mount a female.

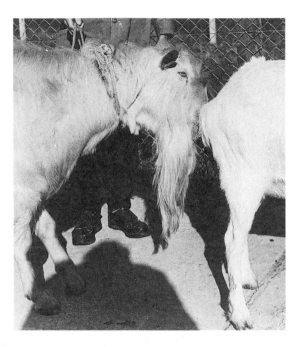

A male may spend a lot of time sniffing and displaying.

ARTIFICIAL INSEMINATION

The problems of finding or keeping a male can be avoided if artificial insemination is used, but unfortunately it is not universally available. Inseminators need special training and the equipment is quite expensive, and the relatively small and dispersed goat population in the UK has made it difficult to develop a viable AI service; it is therefore only available in some areas.

Technically there are no particular problems with using AI with goats. Although it is a little more difficult to process goat semen as compared with that from bulls, it is possible to freeze it in liquid nitrogen, and it appears to remain viable more or less indefinitely.

The technique for inseminating goats involves using a speculum with an in-built light to look down the reproductive tract to see the cervix. Semen is deposited into the neck of the cervix, and sometimes well beyond it.

For the best results it has been found that restraining the goat in a head down, bottom up position is best. Although it looks traumatic for both goat and handler, with experience it is not difficult, and with a competent handler the goats are not distressed – in fact in training sessions for AI technicians a 'practice' goat may well stand around apparently waiting for another go! With good quality semen and an experienced inseminator, a success rate to the first service of around 75 per cent may be achieved.

AI offers all the benefits that the cattle industry has enjoyed for many years, and certainly for the goat keeper with the smaller enterprise, having access to good males, and not having to keep a male, are important advantages.

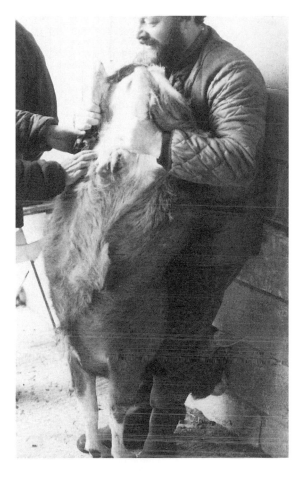

Restraining a female for AI with its head down and bottom up.

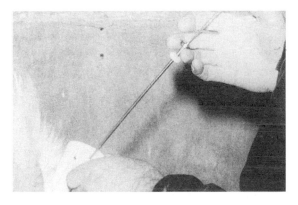

Inseminating through a speculum to deposit semen into the cervix.

GESTATION

Pregnancy in the goat lasts for five months or 150 days; this is just a few days longer than in sheep. If a successful mating has been recorded, it is possible to predict almost exactly the day the goat should kid.

Furthermore in most rural areas there are people who offer a pregnancy detection service using an ultra-sound scanner. Their main business is generally scanning large numbers of sheep, but as goats are so similar to sheep in this respect, they are able to diagnose pregnancy in goats with a high degree of accuracy. The earliest they can reliably do so is around thirty-four days, when they can usually determine the number of foetuses, and will give a fairly accurate estimation of the stage of pregnancy.

A goat that is pregnant is justified in receiving a little more care and attention to maximize the chances of it producing good healthy kids without any trouble. It is important that the prospective mother is adequately, but not overfed. A fat goat can experience a number of problems as the unborn kids or foetuses grow – and even if she doesn't, kidding can often prove difficult for over-fat goats.

Pregnancy is fairly stressful for any animal, and it is a time when diseases and infections that would not be seen at other times, can cause problems. It is important not to add to this stress: for example, avoid moving pregnant goats to a new and unfamiliar environment, or drastically changing their feed, or not allowing them access to adequate shelter during bad weather.

Basically, all this means is that a high standard of husbandry and health care is required if goats are going to get through pregnancy and to kid without problems.

KIDDING

For the novice goat keeper this must be the most anxious, but also the most rewarding aspect of their new reponsibilities. Goats usually kid without problems, but it is important to be ready for any emergency at this time. It is useful to make up a kidding box full of all the things likely to be required. A large plastic toolbox is suitable as it is important that it can be washed from time to time, and that it has a lid that can be fastened shut to keep the contents clean. The kidding box might contain the following items:

> Disposable arm-length gloves
> Obstetric lubricating gel
> Torch
> Paper towel
> Notebook and pen
> Lambing tool
> Lambing cords
> Antiseptic navel spray
> Marker spray
> Ear tags and applicator

The gloves will help prevent the introduction of infection during an assisted kidding, and the gel will be necessary if there are not enough natural fluids to provide lubrication. The torch is vital because problems often occur at night, or at least during the darker hours. Paper towel is always useful to clean hands, the newborn kid if the mother is too weak, or any tools that may have been used. The notebook and pen is included because if more than one kid is born at a time it is often difficult to remember who the mothers are, and in the case of a commercial herd such record keeping is vital as it is likely that there will be many kiddings within a few hours of each other.

The lambing tool is a simple device comprising a 'Y'-shaped plastic tube in which is some plastic cord. The cord is used to help grip the head of a kid inside

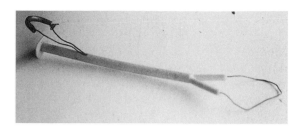

The lambing tool is useful for births where the head needs to be manipulated into the correct position.

its mother during a difficult presentation – often this will allow you to pull it round and into the correct position when hands have failed to do so. The lambing cords are used to help pull the legs of a kid that is proving difficult to deliver. Often kids are so wet and slippery it is almost impossible to get sufficient grip on them to be able to pull them out, and after a long and difficult labour the mother may have given up trying to push them out.

There is a real risk of the newborn kid picking up infection through the navel or umbilicus; if this does happen, there is often subsequent inflammation and swelling in the leg joints, a condition known as joint ill. This is very difficult to treat, and usually results in permanent lameness if the kid is kept and reared. Spraying the navel at birth with an antiseptic helps to prevent this problem.

The marker spray and ear tags are of particular importance in larger herds where several kids may be born at one time, and where it is important to identify and mark them as soon as possible. Temporarily the mother's number can be sprayed on the side of each kid, but for more permanent marking, ear tags will be used. The mother's number and the kid's ear-tag number can then be entered into the notebook and later into the permanent record system.

Until the novice feels sufficiently confident to cope with a difficult kidding it is important to call in someone who will be able to help, such as another goat keeper, a shepherd or sheep farmer, or the vet. Much damage can be done at this time, which at the worst can result in a dead goat and dead kids. Anyone who is called in to help will appreciate a well equipped kidding box (though a vet will probably bring all the necessary equipment).

It is usually possible to tell that a kidding is about to happen. The female will be anxious and will probably stand in a quiet corner of her pen. She may well scratch at the bedding, and may repeatedly lie down and then get up again. Her udder will be swollen, and if a hand is run over her back above her tail, it may be possible to feel that the pelvis has relaxed to increase the size of the birth canal.

Normally some of the membranes surrounding the foetus will be seen first; these are usually filled with fluid, and look like fluid-filled balloons. Often when these membranes rupture and the fluid is released it is possible to see the emerging kid: in a normal presentation, the first things to be seen will be the nose and front feet. If, however, the goat strains for more than one hour without any apparent progress, she should be examined to make sure the kid is in the correct position – if the head or legs are turned back, she will

not be able to push the kid out. Sometimes, and particularly with older goats, she may be able to push out a kid where just one leg is back, but ideally, for a trouble-free birth, the leg should be pulled forwards. A breech birth, where the kid is coming backwards, is not normally a problem as long as the kid is presented feet first.

In most cases of incorrect presentation it is possible to rectify the situation. However, a lot of damage to both kids and mother can be done by clumsy novices, and it is therefore most important that experienced help is sought if difficulties arise. In this situation, if there are no knowledgeable friends to hand, it is important to call a vet.

As soon as the kid has been born it should be placed close to its mother's nose, and usually she will start to clean it immediately. She will clean and dry it most efficiently, and this will also help to establish the bond between them. One of the most important things to do as soon as the kid is born is to remove any membranes covering its nose; and if the mother is too weak to do this after a difficult kidding, then the handler should do it, and also make sure the kid is breathing correctly.

A normal presentation with the kid's nose and two front feet showing.

The kid is pushed out.

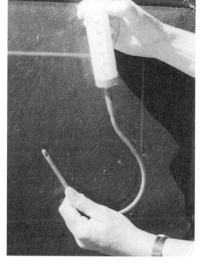

Twins and triplets are quite common in the dairy breeds; this one had quintuplets.

A lamb 'reviver' stomach tube will often save the life of a kid that is too weak to take its first feed.

Young goats kidding for the first time may initially shy away from their newborn kid, but they usually accept them after a few minutes, and will clean them up and 'mother' them most effectively. If there are problems with a mother accepting her kid in a communal pen, she should be penned with her kid or kids in one corner until she is seen to be mothering them. This rarely takes more than twenty-four hours.

If, for any reason, a mother is unable to feed ker kids straightaway, it is most important that they get a feed of warm colostrum (the milk produced immediately after kidding); it is useful to keep some in the deep freeze for such emergencies. If the kid is too weak to suck, it should be fed colostrum via a stomach tube. Small tubes attached to a plastic bottle or syringe are produced for this purpose, and are often sold as 'lamb revivers'. One of these is an extremely useful addition to the kidding equipment, and using one will often transform a kid from being too weak to stand, to one that can seek out its mother and suck from her udder in the normal way.

Goat kids are very precocious, and if healthy, will start to jump and play within a few hours of being born – and in just a few days will be getting into serious mischief!

KEY POINTS

- Normally goats are seasonal breeders that mate in the autumn and kid in the spring.
- Oestrus, or heat, is relatively easy to detect.
- Most people with just a small number of goats use the services of a stud male.
- A limited AI service is available in the UK.
- Kidding can be more traumatic for the handler than for the goats. Experienced advice should be sought at this time.
- Goats often have twins or triplets, and are usually good mothers.
- Kids are very precocious and soon get into mischief.

5   Rearing Kids————————

The first practical question to be asked regarding the rearing of kids is: 'Will there be a use for them if they are reared?' As with all pet animals, there are a great many that are not wanted, and in the case of goats, particularly males. Goat kids are very appealing, and there is a natural desire to rear them, even though they may well be unwanted as adults. There is only a very limited goat meat market in the UK, and rearing male kids for meat is rarely financially viable. (This aspect is discussed in Chapters 8 and 11.)

If the kids are to be reared there are two options: to leave them with their mother until they are old enough to be weaned; or to rear them 'artificially' using a milk substitute. Which method is chosen will depend on whether or not the milk is required for sale: if it is, then the average value of goat's milk makes rearing using a milk replacer a very economic alternative. If the milk is not to be sold, then leaving the kids with their mothers is by far the simplest rearing system.

Whatever system is used, it is important that the kids receive a good feed of colostrum from their mother during the first few days after birth. The kids should be checked regularly to make sure they are strong and well. Normally goat kids are extremely precocious and very active within a few hours of birth, so any kid that spends most of the time lying down, or when up and about is constantly crying, should be investigated. If its stomach appears to be empty and/or it seems to be hungry, it is important to find out why: the mother may not have any milk, she may have an udder infection (usually called mastitis), or she may have simply rejected the kid. If none of these seems to be the case it is possible that there is something wrong with the kid.

It may be necessary to feed it via a stomach tube or 'lamb reviver', as described in the previous chapter. And if after a feed of warm colostrum it still does not appear to be well, it may be necessary to put it down (euthanaze it) in order to prevent any further suffering.

HOUSING KIDS

Kids are very active and adventurous, so any pen that they are kept in must be very carefully constructed if they are not to escape and end up wandering around the farm or garden. Hurdles covered with welded mesh make good barriers. It is also important to make sure there is nothing in the pen which could be used as a 'launching pad', because kids love to jump up onto things that provide a firm surface above ground level, such as hayracks, water troughs, feeders and window ledges. If the pen is so constructed that the mother can put her head out to feed and drink from buckets hanging on the outside of the pen, then it is highly likely that the kids will be able to get out through the openings, too.

Apart from being escape-proof, the pen must also provide a healthy environment for the kids to grow normally. The first requirement is good ventilation without draughts: a nice airy shed, with plenty of air space and sufficient openings to give plenty of air changes. Unfortunately many old farm buildings, old garages and garden sheds have relatively low roofs, and these will not give enough air space unless they are very open; they could also easily result in respiratory disease in the kids.

Kids seek attention and company, and if they are to be reared 'artificially' it is better if they can be in groups. The problem for the smaller scale goat keeper is that he is unlikely to have many kids born at any one time; and if only one kid is born, it is kinder to leave it with its mother. If, however, there are enough to rear them in groups, they seem to do best if the group sizes are not too large for the first two months – eight to ten seems to be a good size. It is also important to try to keep kids of similar size together. One small kid in a pen of larger ones will rarely get its fair share of food, and will almost certainly remain smaller than the rest for a long time.

About 0.6sq m (6sq ft) of space should be allowed per kid. A square pen constructed from four conventional 6ft (1.8m) hurdles would be suitable for six kids. The pen should be kept dry; it will need cleaning out weekly, particularly once the kids are drinking a lot of milk as, not surprisingly, they will produce a lot of urine.

FEEDING

If the kids are to be reared artificially they will need a substitute for their mother's milk. Goat's milk and cow's milk are very similar in composition, and so if a supply of cow's milk can be bought at farm (wholesale) price, this may be the most economic alternative. A milk replacer powder formulated for calves would also be suitable, and there is a bewildering range of these. If low-cost rearing is important, those made from whey powder without skimmed milk are usually the cheapest.

Different goat keepers will have different priorities. If it is important to rear the kids for least cost, then the system used will involve feeding a less expensive milk powder for the shortest time possible – between six and eight weeks.

Whichever system is used, the kids will need a feeder from which they can drink the milk or milk substitute. For those with the task of rearing just one or two kids, a bottle with a teat is the simplest method of feeding. However, feeding even two kids can take a while, and if time is limited, a feeder that allows the kids to feed themselves would be useful. The simplest type of self-feeder is one where one or more bottles can be fixed and left for the kids to help themselves. It may take a few days for the kids to learn to feed satisfactorily, but once they do, it is much less time-consuming than holding the bottles for them!

If larger numbers of kids are to be reared, then some form of multi-teat feeder may be used. These usually consist of a vessel or container with teats sticking

A simple rack for holding feeder bottles will save a lot of time.

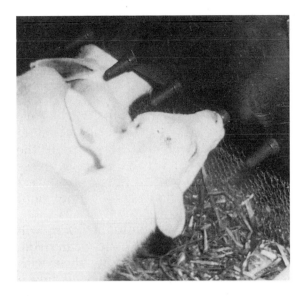

Kids drinking milk replacer from a multi-teat feeder.

rate will be much slower – but then the cost will be correspondingly lower.

Most people find that, taking everything into consideration, early weaning and teaching the kids to eat solid food is preferable – and when the kids are considered over, say, the first six months of life, ultimately this regime does not seem to affect growth rate very much: basically, kids that are weaned on to solid food early tend to catch up with respect to growth, and eventually will be indistinguishable from kids that consume much more milk before they are weaned.

There will be mixing instructions on all bags of milk replacer. Some are best mixed and fed warm, and some can be fed cold. Generally speaking, the milk replacers that are fed cold are most appropriate for ad lib systems because it is difficult to

out, or one where the teats have small pipes or tubes through which the milk is sucked up, similar to a child's drinking straw. The ones with the teat directly in the milk are easier for the kids to drink from, but have the disadvantage of losing all the milk if the teat leaks. This can often happen as the kids get older, because they are very likely to chew holes in the teats, or to simply pull them out.

There are various options for feeding regimes. Many goat keepers will choose to bottle-feed their goats for much longer than is necessary because they find it such an enjoyable task, and they think that just because the kids demand milk, they need it. Basically the choice is between ad-lib feeding, or feeding the kids a predetermined ration.

Ad-lib feeding will be more expensive because the kids will consume a lot of milk or milk substitute before they are weaned. However, this also means they usually grow faster and reach a good weight by the time they are weaned. If, on the other hand, the milk ration is limited, particularly if it is minimal, the growth

A Suitable Regime for Ad Lib Feeding		
Weeks	**milk quantity**	**number of feeds per day**
1–6	ad lib (just clearing up)	2
7	half amount consumed last day of week 6	1
8	half last day of wk 7	1
9	no milk	

A Regime for Feeding a Rationed Amount of Milk		
Weeks	**milk quantity**	**number of feeds per day**
1–7	1 litre/day	2
8	0.5 litres/day	1
9	no milk	

keep milk warm for long periods. Also, when warm milk is available ad lib, kids tend to drink too much at one time. They rarely do this with cold milk, and will tend to drink small amounts often.

Having said that, it is much easier to teach kids to drink from any type of feeder if the milk is warm. If a ration of milk feed is given, it is possible to offer this in an open vessel such as a small plastic trough or box. DIY stores often sell small storage boxes made from strong plastic, and some of these make good kid troughs.

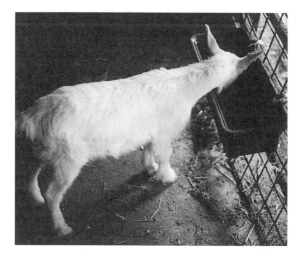

A kid drinking a ration of milk from a plastic trough.

It takes time and patience to teach kids to drink, and the longer they are left with their mothers, the harder this becomes. If the goat milk is required for sale, then the kids should be taken from their mothers at four days of age, which is when colostrum production has finished and the milk can be sold. Most milk replacers seem to be quite palatable, and as long as the kids like the taste, they can usually be persuaded to drink after a few hours of hunger. If they refuse to drink, it often helps to put a milky finger into their mouth to make sure they can taste the milk.

It is important to have feeders at the correct height. Kids naturally want to feed from above, and it takes a little time to teach them to put their heads down into a trough. The trough needs to be as high as possible, the main proviso being that the kids can get their heads in to drink. The milk in a trough positioned at a higher level will not be fouled as easily as one close to the floor.

Once the kids are drinking well, rearing is relatively straightforward; however, a high standard of husbandry and hygiene is required to keep them healthy. Milk feeders should be cleaned out between every feed, and the pens should also be cleaned regularly, and fresh straw added almost daily. During the first few weeks, before the kids start eating much solid food, the bedding in the pens will quickly become wet.

Concentrate feed in the form of calf- or lamb-rearing pellets, with a crude protein content of 18–20 per cent, should be offered from the beginning of the rearing period, although the kids will actually eat very little until they are two to three weeks old. This concentrate feed should be provided in a feeder that the kids cannot climb into – although in fact this is easier said than done, because if they can get their heads in, they can usually get their bodies in as well! However, with a little ingenuity it is possible to make a feeder that works fairly well out of an old plastic container.

Hay should also be offered, although this should be no more than a small handful until the kids are eating plenty of pellets. If the kids have free access to hay they will probably eat this in preference to the concentrate feed, to the detriment of their growth rate.

Clean water should be provided at all times. Even when kids are drinking milk they will often drink water, and this should be encouraged, as it will help them in the change to solid food.

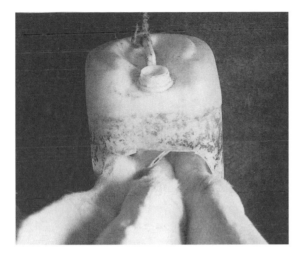

A home-made feeder for concentrate pellets which only very small kids would be able to climb into.

Free access to hay is only given after the kids are eating plenty of solid feed.

There is no hard and fast rule about when to wean. If the kids are doing particularly well and are eating plenty of solid food, they can be weaned off the milk feed at six to seven weeks of age. If they are left with their mothers they will be weaned naturally at three to five months of age – but again, they can be separated as soon as they are seen to be eating significant amounts of solid food.

Whatever their age when they are separated from their mothers, it is kinder to move them far enough away so they cannot hear each other.

MARKING KIDS

Those with just a few goats may consider marking for identification unnecessary. However, if they are all the same colour, as Saanens, it is often difficult to tell them apart, and whatever the level of interest, it is good to know who is related to whom. Coloured marker sprays from any agricultural supplies store are useful for temporary identification; for a more permanent system a collar with a disc or tag is a simple method – although these may well be destroyed later when the goats are full grown, when they will chew anything that adorns their companions. The more commercially minded goat keeper is advised to use one of the many ear-tagging systems available for lambs.

If the kids are pedigree and are to be registered with the British Goat Society or the British Angora Goat Society they have to be marked by a tattoo in their ear. In this case the mark will include a letter or letters designating the herd, the kid's

A kid sprayed with its mother's number.

own number, and a letter showing the year of birth. Tattooing equipment may be considered too expensive for someone with only a few kids to register each year, especially as many local goat clubs often have equipment which they will lend out; also, sometimes a club member will tattoo other members' kids.

DISBUDDING

For goats kept in fairly close confinement, such as in small pens or paddocks, horns have many disadvantages and virtually no advantages, especially if the goats will be handled frequently. The worst situation is to have one or two horned goats amongst others that are not. The horned ones will be very bossy, and invariably will not let the others have adequate access to feed or shelter. They may even become aggressive towards their handler – and even if they are not actually aggressive, there is still the potential for accidental injury.

Certain breeds, such as Pygmies and Angoras, are usually left with their horns, but as long as they all have horns there are few problems; although in the case of Pygmies, handling problems may develop with individual males.

Disbudding of goat kids in the UK must be carried out by a veterinarian. It is much more difficult to anaesthetize the nerves to the horn buds of a kid than to those of a calf, and usually a general anaesthetic is used. Disbudding should be carried out as soon as possible after birth; if the kids are more than two weeks of age the horn buds are often so large they need cutting off before the hot iron is applied.

It becomes more difficult to stop horn growth completely the older the kid is at the time of disbudding. It is important that a very hot disbudding iron is used; those heated in a flame are much more effective than electrically heated ones.

CASTRATION

Not many people will need to castrate male kids because they will not be kept until they are mature: either they will be killed for meat, or they will be put down at birth. However, if a male kid is to be kept for more than six months for any other reason than breeding, it should be castrated. The preferred method is with a rubber ring or 'elastrator', applied within the first week of life. In the first instance instruction should be sought from either an experienced goat keeper or a sheep farmer. If there is good reason for the castration of older kids, this must be done surgically by a veterinarian, under anaesthesia.

The scrotum of a five-day-old kid.

The rubber ring stretched by the 'elastrator' tool.

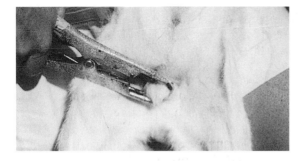

The ring is placed over the scrotum.

Goat kids have been known to mate successfully at three months of age and therefore, if entire male kids are to be kept, they must be separated from the female kids before this.

KEY POINTS

- Should the kids be reared? Will they be required when adult?
- Uncastrated male kids should not be reared unless they are required for breeding, or if they are to be used for meat at an early age.
- Kids can be reared economically on milk replacer if their mother's milk is required for sale or for processing.
- If the kids are to be registered they must be ear-marked with a tattoo.
- All female dairy kids should be disbudded within a week of birth. Horns are a problem with housed goats.

6 Milk Production and Dairy Work

The dairy goat can produce impressive quantities of milk, and in fact produces far more than a cow if appropriate breeds and environments are compared. Almost certainly this means that anyone keeping a female goat will at some point be faced with the task of milking, and will probably have to cope with more milk than an average family can drink. This in turn leads to an interest in how to process it, whether into cheese, yoghurt or other dairy products; several commercial cheese and yoghurt producers came into business this way.

It has always been considered an unavoidable fact of life that dairy farmers should do the milking at unearthly hours in order to achieve an even twelve-hour interval between the two daily milkings in order to maximize yields. Research suggests that this may not be as critical as many of them think – though it is a fact that if the udder becomes engorged with milk, the back pressure created will have an inhibitory effect on the milk production of the glandular tissue. The good news is that the anatomy of a goat udder is a little different from that of the cow.

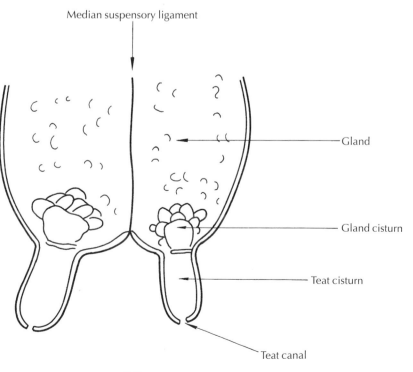

A cross-section of a goat's udder showing the cistern which stores milk until it is sucked out by the kid or the milking machine.

Median suspensory ligament

Gland

Gland cisturn

Teat cisturn

Teat canal

An udder or mammary gland is made up of the glandular tissue which produces the milk; a space or chamber called the cistern where a certain amount of milk is stored; a teat cistern, which is another chamber in the teat itself; and then a teat canal through which the milk leaves the udder. In a goat udder the cistern capacity is greater than in a cow udder, and it would appear that it takes longer to create inhibitory back pressure. This means that unequal milking intervals will have a less deleterious effect on milk yield – though it would be unwise to leave high-yielding goats unmilked for more than sixteen hours.

HAND MILKING

Most people with just a few goats will hand milk them, rather than invest in relatively expensive machines. Hand milking can be a very pleasant task if the goat co-operates, which they generally do, but it has to be done twice a day for nine or ten months of the year, and it can prove to be quite a chore. Furthermore it can lead to premature ageing of finger and wrist joints if too much is done on a regular basis.

The action of hand milking is remarkably similar to what the kid does when it sucks milk from the udder. When a kid feeds from its mother it traps milk in the teat cistern with its tongue and hard palate and then presses it out of the teat. When it relaxes its jaw the cistern refills, and it then squeezes again. To hand milk a goat the forefinger and thumb are used to trap milk in the teat cistern, and then the other fingers squeeze, in a cascading fashion, forcing the milk out of the teat. Trying this for the first time often produces no milk at all, or at best a most unimpressive tiny spurt! However, with a little practice on a tolerant goat, hand milking can soon result in a quick milking

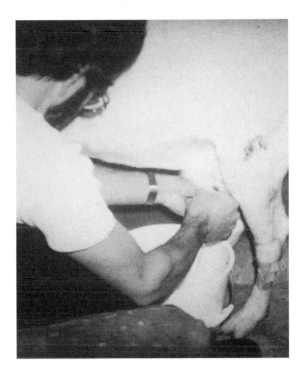

Hand milking into a clean bucket on a clean floor.

out – in fact a skilled milker will work so quickly that the milk will rattle into the bucket in a steady stream, and by the time they have finished there will be a layer of froth on the milk.

Hygiene is of paramount importance when hand milking, as there are plenty of opportunities for the milk to become contaminated. Ideally a stainless steel bucket should be used, as plastic becomes scratched and is then difficult to clean to the standard required. Everyone who produces milk for sale must be registered under the Dairy Products (Hygiene) Regulations 1995, and one of the fundamental requirements is that goats should be milked in a separate air space to the one in which they live. Even producers who produce milk solely for their own consumption are advised to adopt this practice, as milk in open containers can be so easily contaminated by airborne bacteria.

Goats that have just kidded should be 'eased out' if their udders are tight, in spite of feeding the kids – sometimes if the udder is very tight this is necessary to enable the kids to feed. If not taken by the kid, the colostrum or first milk, which lasts for four days after kidding, should be discarded. This is particularly important if the milk is to be used for the manufacture of cheese, as the bactericidal properties of the colostrum may interfere with the cheese-making process.

MACHINE MILKING

As already discussed, hand milking carries a greater risk of comtamination, and anyone with more than five or six goats should consider machine milking. The simplest machine-milking systems are those using a portable vacuum pump and buckets into which the milk is drawn. Normally these portable units can milk two or four goats at one time depending on the size of pump. The vacuum pump, driven by an electric or internal combustion motor, is often mounted on a trolley, and thus the goats can be milked almost anywhere.

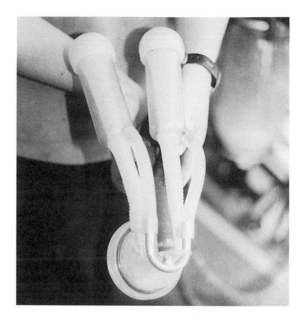

The cluster on a goat milking machine showing transparent plastic shells and silicone rubber liners.

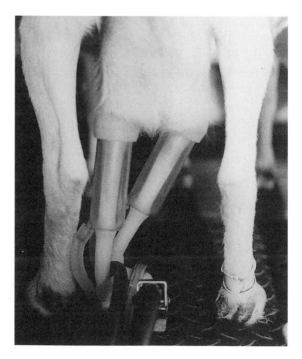

A mobile milking unit (Fullwood Ltd) will allow goats to be machine milked anywhere.

The cluster in use on a machine where the goats are milked from behind.

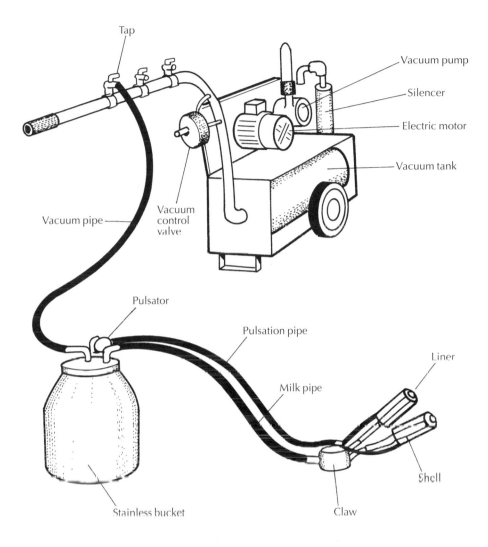

Tap

Vacuum pump

Silencer

Electric motor

Vacuum tank

Vacuum pipe

Vacuum control valve

Pulsator

Pulsation pipe

Liner

Milk pipe

Shell

Stainless bucket

Claw

The main components of a mobile milking unit.

A milking machine works by creating a vacuum which, when applied to the goat's teats, draws the milk out through the milking unit; this unit comprises shells, liners, and a bowl or claw piece, which together make up what is called the cluster. A device called a pulsator creates a pulse in the vacuum which allows the liner to relax around the teat in a rythmic fashion. If a continuous vacuum were applied to the teat it would interfere with the circulation of blood, and the teat would become very red in the way our own skin will if we suck hard on a small area for a short time. With a portable bucket system a vacuum is created in the buckets, and the milk is drawn into them. At some convenient point as the bucket becomes full, it is emptied through a filter into a churn or other vessel, where the milk can then be cooled.

Larger installations will have fixed equipment where the milk is transferred along pipes, sometimes via recording jars, into a receiver jar from where it is pumped into a refrigerated storage or bulk tank. It

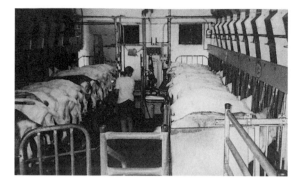

Thirty-six goats standing in the milking parlour at the Water Farm Goat Centre.

is important to point out at this juncture that it is possible to damage goats' milk at this stage. If it is moved around too much this activity may break up the fat, a process called lipolysis, and the result will be the release of fatty acids, some of which can cause very unpleasant taints in the milk. There are also enzymes in the milk that will do the same thing, paticularly when it is warm, and so it is most important to cool the milk effectively down to 4°C if unpleasant taints are to be avoided. Inadequate cooling is the most common cause of unpleasant taints in goat milk, and is why so many people have had bad experiences when tasting goats' milk for the first time. If correctly produced and cooled, goats' milk should taste similar to cows' milk, without any 'off' flavours or taints.

Goats are very clean animals whose udders are rarely dirty, and normally they produce very clean milk with a very low bacteria count. If cooled correctly, immediately after milking and then stored at 4°C, goats' milk will keep well and can be used for processing after two to three days. In machine-milked systems, particularly those where the milk travels through

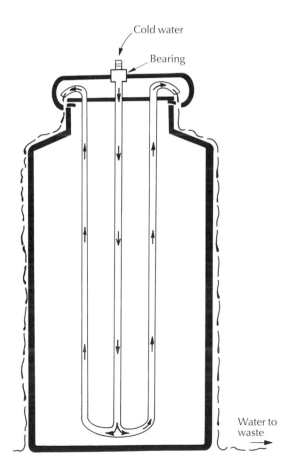

Showing the flow of cold water through an in-churn cooler.

An in-churn milk cooler (Fullwood Ltd).

pipes, there is less risk of contaminating the milk with airborne bacteria than there is with hand milking into open buckets.

CLEANING MILKING EQUIPMENT

Whichever system is used, it is most important that all surfaces that come into contact with milk are thoroughly and correctly cleaned. Buckets used for hand milking, and small-scale portable milking machines, will be cleaned by hand; however, the principles are the same for all equipment. Milk residues are washed

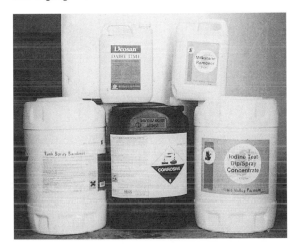

Some dairy chemicals used for cleaning milking equipment.

An in-churn filter which uses disposable paper filter pads.

away with cold water as soon as possible after milking, and then the equipment is washed with a hot solution of any one of a number of approved dairy cleaning chemicals.

After all surfaces have been thoroughly washed with this, they are rinsed with a weak hypochlorite solution and are then left to drain and dry ready for the next milking. It is important that the equipment can dry because bacteria will often multiply on wet surfaces, and sometimes even in disinfectant solutions that have been used for cleaning. For the same reasons all cleaning tools, such as brushes, should be hung up to dry after use.

DAIRY WORK

It is not appropriate in this book to go into great detail about dairy work and the processing of milk into dairy products: it is a specialized subject, and many good books have been written to help the amateur or professional with the processes that are involved. However, as it is almost inevitable that dairy goat owners will become interested in this aspect, some information has been included here to at least help them make decisions about how much they want to become involved.

Most people who keep dairy goats, even those that are just pets, inevitably end up producing milk, and they are then faced with the problem of what to do with the surplus. It would be quite normal for a goat of no particular quality to produce 5–6 litres (9–10 pints) of milk, and this is usually much more than the average family will consume in a day. However, a great deal of pleasure can be gained by turning raw milk into dairy products such as cheese, yoghurt, cream, ice-cream or butter. Note that new legislation makes it difficult to make such products for sale, as generally it is necessary to be processing on a fairly large scale to justify the investment needed to create the correct conditions.

The Dairy

If the intention is to process milk to make products for sale it is important to realize that the law requires high standards in the dairy to ensure the safety of the products and the health of those who will consume them. The conditions required are set out in the Dairy Products Legislation of 1995. Even if milk is being processed for home consumption it is still advisable to adopt the principles set down in this legislation, as there are real risks to health from consuming dairy products that have been produced in unsatisfactory conditions.

As with the milking area, the first requirement is for the dairy to be away from the area in which the goats live. Ideally it should be as close as possible to the milking area to avoid having to move the milk too far. A very high standard of hygiene is required, and it is therefore very important that the dairy can be cleaned correctly and kept clean; this means having impervious washable surfaces, which could be an impervious paint over rendering or glazed tiles. Good drainage is also important, as any puddles left on any surface are a potential source of bacteria. No other food preparation should go on in the dairy room, and therefore processing in the kitchen is not recommended, and in fact would not be allowed under the Dairy Regulations.

DAIRY PRODUCTS

The simplest dairy product is milk for drinking. Goats' milk is the subject of many myths regarding its properties and characteristics, most of them untrue. If

produced in clean, hygienic circumstances, and if it is correctly cooled immediately after milking, goats' milk should be delicious like any other milk, and should not have any unpleasant tastes or taints.

It does not have any magical properties that will bring about cures of certain illnesses, as some folk lore would suggest. It is, however, a useful substitute for those who show allergy or intolerance to cows' milk. Although the two milks are remarkably similar, there are small differences in the levels of the various casein fractions that are probably the reason why about 75 per cent of those allergic to cows' milk do not show the same allergy to goats' milk.

This difference has been responsible for some remarkable 'cures' in infants with conditions such as eczema and asthma. If these are the manifestation of an allergy to cows' milk, replacing the cows' milk with goats' milk may be all that is needed.

One special property of goats' milk is that it seems to be more easily digested than most other milks. For this reason the goat was often called 'the universal foster mother'. People with digestive problems such as ulcers often find they can cope with goats' milk but not cows' milk.

In the same way as cows' milk, it has a different composition to human milk, and should not be fed to babies without prior medical advice.

Pasteurization

There are many diseases that can be transmitted to humans via milk, and normally pasteurization is recommended to reduce the risk of these. Some people contend that unpasteurized milk is more wholesome than pasteurized, but experimental evidence shows that the nutritional value of milk is not adversely affected by the pasteurization process, and this, coupled with the possible risks from unpasteurized milk, make a fairly convincing argument.

In the pasteurization process the milk is heated to a specific temperature for a specific time in order to kill most of the potentially harmful bacteria. There are two principal methods of pasteurization: one involves heating a batch or vat of milk to 63°C for 30 minutes; the other, often called 'high temperature, short time' (HTST), involves heating the milk to 72.5°C for 15 seconds. This latter method is usually carried out using a continuous flow, heated plate type of pasteurizer. Small quantities of milk can be pasteurized by heating the milk in a double boiler – a pan that is inside another filled with water and heated over a cooker.

If the milk is being processed for sale, it is cartonned after pasteurization and cooling. It is important that it is put into cartons or bottles that can be sealed to be airtight; if it is not, bacteria will contaminate the milk and adversely affect its keeping qualities. The cost of the correct carton- or bottle-filling and sealing equipment would be too expensive for small-scale producers. Small, hand-operated filling machines are available, but the combination of slowness of operation and cost makes it difficult to produce drinking milk profitably on a small scale.

In the past, a lot of milk was sold for drinking that was unpasteurized; it was often packaged in plastic bags or sachets which were then deep frozen. This system is not used so much now, as most people recognize the potential risks from raw milk; also the frozen bags of milk are difficult to handle and store.

Goat keepers producing milk just for their own consumption will almost certainly think that it is not worth going to all the trouble involved in pasteurization. Certainly if the goats are healthy and a high standard of hygiene is observed during and after milking, and if the milk is regularly tested for bacterial quality, the risks can be minimized.

Yoghurt

The first yoghurt was made from goats' milk many centuries ago. It is now one of the most popular dairy goat products, and was one of the first to find a place on supermarket shelves. Basically yoghurt is milk that has been modified by the action of bacteria, which improves its keeping qualities. The bacteria now used are *Lactobacillus bulgaricus* and *Streptobacillus thermophilus*, and they are added to warm milk as a starter culture; at the amateur level, another 'live' yoghurt can

Cartons of pasteurized goats' milk.

Yoghurt was first made from goats' milk.

be used. The milk is then incubated at a temperature between 37.5°C and 45°C.

Incubation can be carried out with the yoghurt already in pots, or it can be done with the culture in a heated vat. The yoghurt should set in six to eight hours, and it is then transferred to a refrigerator. A bewildering range of flavourings are available for those who find unflavoured and unsweetened yoghurt a little too sour. For those wishing to sell yoghurt it should be noted that there are very strict rules and regulations about labelling such products, and as these regulations seem to be constantly changing, expert advice on labelling and packaging should be sought.

Cheese

About 75 per cent of the goats' milk produced in the UK is used for the manufacture of cheese. Cheeses can be grouped into five main types: fresh, soft, blue, hard and whey, and the form the cheese takes results from the way it is made, and how it is stored after manufacture. All cheese starts off as milk that has curdled and which has then had some of the liquid drained or squeezed out of it. The starters that are used to make cheese are *lactobacilli* which cause the casein in the milk to coagulate, and rennet which causes the structure known as 'casein mycelles' to group together to form a sort of mat which traps the other solids in the milk. The starters that are used, and the degree of coagulation that is achieved, will give the cheese its particular characteristics. Further differences are achieved by different levels of liquid or whey removal, and by different maturing times and conditions.

Fresh cheese is made by hanging curd in a bag for a short time to drain off some of the whey, before placing it in a mould for a short time. It is usually eaten just a few hours after it has been made.

Soft cheese is made in much the same way, but it is drained for longer and is then left to ripen for five to thirty days. The characteristics of the cheese will depend on the ripening time and the bacteria culture that has been used. Any cheese made from unpasteurized milk will be much more variable, as many naturally occurring bacteria will influence the curd formation and its flavour. It is difficult to make a cheese with consistent characteristics from unpasteurized milk.

Blue cheese is made by inoculating the blocks of curd with the blue mould *Penicillum glaucum*, after which they are ripened for up to five months in a controlled environment at a temperature of 9–10°C and a relative humidity of 90–95 per cent. It is important that other cheeses are not ripened in the same room as blue cheese, because the blue mould may contaminate these.

Hard goats' cheese is produced by squeezing out most of the liquid from the curd, usually by using some form of press. The curd is pressed in moulds, and these will give the finished cheese its shape, which in most cases will be cylindrical. The cheeses may be salted, and they are then wrapped in muslin cheesecloths before being placed in a controlled environment store – years ago this was often the farmhouse cellar. Some mature cheeses may be left to ripen for more than twelve months.

Cream

Compared to cows' milk, the fat in goats' milk is made up of a larger proportion of small globules, and this makes it more difficult to separate the cream. Most cream separators need to be set to the finest adjustment, and often it is necessary to put the milk through the separator twice to get a reasonable yield of cream. Because of these problems, very few processing dairies make goats' cream.

A small, hand-operated cream separator (Fullwood Ltd).

A small, electrically operated butter churn (Fullwood Ltd)

Butter

The problems of making cream are much the same for butter, and again, not much goats' milk butter is made. Unless colouring is added, goats' milk butter is particularly white due to the lack of carotene pigments in the milk. Small butter separators are now available for the smaller producer, and it would certainly be practical for someone with just a few milking goats to produce enough butter for home consumption.

Ice Cream

Ice cream made from goats' milk is delicious, but producers find some resistance until they have persuaded people to try it for the first time. It is an attractive product as it is not difficult to make, and if good outlets can be developed, a high return can be achieved from a given quantity of milk. Once again, anyone thinking of selling ice cream commercially should be aware of the mass of regulations concerning hygiene, packaging and labelling.

MARKETING DAIRY PRODUCE

As already mentioned, there are a great many prejudices regarding goats' milk, very often as a result of poor quality products being sold to those trying goat products for the first time. On balance it is probably a good thing that legislation has made it difficult for all but the most dedicated to produce and sell dairy products on a small scale. The fact that all producers and processors have to be licensed under the Dairy Products legislation should go a long way to ensuring that only good quality products are offered for sale.

Once all the legal aspects have been dealt with regarding hygiene, packaging and labelling, producers can concentrate on how best to reach the large potential market for speciality dairy products.

Attractive packaging, image and presentation are as important as the quality of the products itself. However, if someone is persuaded to try a new product for the first time and they do not like it, they will probably not buy from that source again, even if different products are made.

Once the first sales have been achieved, the next most important aspect is continuity. It must be possible to guarantee a certain level of supply, however small, and the product must be consistently good. A buyer, whether a small shop proprietor or a supermarket buyer, will not be very interested in a product that is variable, and that is only available intermittently.

The whole subject of marketing is probably the one that most justifies calling in professional advice. Most goat keepers and farmers will be unfamiliar with marketing tricks of the trade, and as already discussed, the legal aspects are becoming more and more important and are forever changing, making it difficult for all but the specialist to keep up to date.

KEY POINTS

- Milking goats can produce in excess of 9l (2 gal) of milk per day, and need milking twice a day for 305 days.
- Anyone with more than two to three goats should invest in a milking machine.
- Anyone planning to sell goats' milk must register with MAFF.
- Hygiene is most important when producing milk for sale or for home consumption.
- Goats' milk is a useful substitute for cows' milk, and often in cases of allergy does not result in the same reaction.
- Goats' milk can be used for all milk products such as cheese, yoghurt, cream and ice cream.
- It would be foolish to commence serious milk production without establishing a market for it.

7 Fibre Goats and Fibre Production—

Although goat hair has almost certainly been used for as long as goats have been domesticated, it is only comparatively recently that the interest in its production has been revived in the UK. In the early 1980s a few Angora goats were imported from Tasmania and New Zealand, and these created a great deal of interest: soon, it seemed, everyone wanted some, and the resulting demand forced up the price of breeding stock to unprecedented heights. This encouraged others to look at the production of other goat fibre, and soon there was also an interest in cashmere goats.

ANGORA GOATS

Angora goats are natives of Turkey where they are farmed in quite large numbers for their hair, which is called mohair. They were highly prized, and none were allowed out of Turkey until 1838 when some were exported to South Africa; these became the foundation of what is now the most important mohair-producing country in the world.

Angora goats are nearly always white, although some colour variations do occur. Their coat of mohair grows at the rate of about 2.5cm (1in) a month, and they are shorn twice a year. Thus their appearance will differ according to the time of year: newly shorn they look a little like sheep; with a few months' growth their fleece will hang down in curls or ringlets – if it is parted, the mohair underneath the usually grubby outer layer will be seen to be white and lustrous.

Angora goats are usually horned, and unlike dairy goats, the horns are left to grow. With the more extensive type of husbandry practised with Angoras, the horns have no major disadvantages and they do give something to hold on to; without them there would be a temptation to hold onto the fleece, which is not a good practice.

Angora goats never seem to be quite as inquisitive as dairy goats, and in fact in some ways seem to have more in common with sheep. They do, however, have the goat's typical appetite for a wider range of plant species than sheep, and will do the same good job of tidying up rough grazing.

They are normally kept outdoors, and from an economic point of view a commercial farmer would not be able to justify keeping them housed in the same way as dairy goats because the financial return per goat is so much less. They are quite hardy, and as long as they have access to a building for shelter, and if the ground does not become too wet and muddy, they can be kept out throughout the year.

During the winter months when the grass is not growing, Angoras that are out to grass should be given hay daily. They should also be given a little concentrate feed at times of high demand, normally in late pregnancy and early lactation. How much to give must be carefully worked

Mohair fleeces will be less contaminated if low-level hay racks are used.

out, because if they are fed too much concentrate they will tend to put on fat, and as a consequence of this could have problems mating and kidding, and then the quality of the fleece – the mohair – could be adversely affected.

Housing would be justified if the weather was really bad, and particularly if this was after they had been shorn – one shearing is bound to be during the winter. Housing need not be much more than a roof over their heads, and enough side protection to stop the prevailing weather blowing onto them or the bedding of their pens. As with dairy goats, walls to just above their body height, and windbreak plastic mesh above this, provide a good compromise between shelter and ventilation.

They will be fed hay while housed, and it is preferable that this should be in low-level racks as they will tend to contaminate their fleeces with hay seeds and dust and debris if they are pulling it down from high level racks suspended from walls or the sides of their pens.

HARVESTING AND MARKETING MOHAIR

Angora goats are unusual in that their main coat is made up of what would normally be secondary fibre from secondary follicles. Most goats have a coat comprising primary outer hair from primary follicles, and secondary hair which grows down under the main coat.

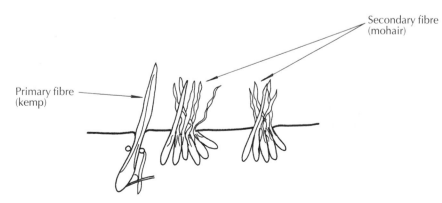

Mohair grows from secondary follicles.

Primary hairs do exist in mohair, and these are called kemp fibres; however, they are considered undesirable, as too high a proportion of kemp will down-value the mohair.

Mohair is very fine, with kid mohair up to 30 microns (a micron is 1/1,000mm) and mohair from an adult buck around 40 microns. To put this into perspective, human hair is usually in the range 50–60 microns. Mohair also has 'lustre', meaning that it shines, because the scales of the hair – which can only be seen under a microscope – are larger, and lie much flatter than on wool: they reflect the light, causing the characteristic lustre.

The best Angora goats are those with the best compromise between total weight of fleece and fineness, and with no kemp. The thickness of the fibres can be determined to some extent visually. Coarse mohair tends to be straighter than fine, which will lie in curls and tight ringlets; ideally the goat should have the same type of mohair growing evenly over its entire body. As they get older there is a tendency for coarser hair to grow around the breast and forelegs. Virtually no kemp fibres should be present, but if they are,

they will be along the top line and on the head between the horns. They can be recognized by pulling out a pinch of hair and laying it over a dark surface such as the sleeve of a dark sweater or overall. The kemp fibres will show up against the dark background as coarse, chalky, lustreless fibres amongst the finer mohair.

As already mentioned, Angora goats are normally shorn twice a year because mohair grows at the rate of about 2.5cm (1in) a month, and the ideal length for processing it is when it is about 15cm (6in). The best time to shear them is just before kidding in the spring, and just before mating in the autumn: kidding is cleaner and therefore less troublesome, and the kids have less trouble finding the teats when the mohair is short; and when in season the goats will mate more

The technique for shearing Angora goats is similar to that for sheep.

An adult male Angora goat showing coarse mohair.

Angora goats just after the spring shearing.

desirable parts will be put into separate bags. Thus different bags will be used for hair that is badly soiled, hair that appears coarser than the rest, and hair that may be from areas with more kemp fibres. When mohair is sold in Bradford, the historical home of almost all animal fibre processing in the UK, buyers will sample bags or bales, and will pay according to the quality of the sample. This means it is important that the bags or bales containing the best quality mohair do not contain anything else, because if poor quality fibre were to get into the bag and be sampled, then the whole bag would be down-valued.

Those thinking of producing mohair on a large scale, or who do not wish to get involved in processing, will either sell it through British Mohair Marketing, a co-operative set up by the British Angora Goat Society, or they will liaise with someone who is processing and crafting mohair into finished garments.

Most people associate mohair with fluffy sweaters, but it is a very versatile fibre that has many applications. One of its many qualities is that it has a great affinity for dye, and does not easily fade: this has made it suitable for high quality curtains, carpeting and upholstery velours.

For the same reason it is also used for the manufacture of hoods and tonneau covers for some of the more expensive open motor cars, and also for good quality suiting and skirting cloth, judges' wigs, paint rollers and ski bindings.

As with dairy goats, there is always the opportunity for the small-scale producer to process the raw product themselves. Once washed and combed, the mohair can be dyed and spun into yarn and used for hand-crafted garments which, if well made, will sell well in tourist areas where people are keen to purchase locally crafted products.

successfully when free of their dense, heavy fleece.

Shearing Angora goats is not very different to shearing sheep, and an experienced sheep shearer will therefore manage quite well. The main differences are that mohair is much finer than wool, and this means a finer comb must be used on the shearing machine otherwise the cutting head will get too hot; for the same reason a slower machine speed is necessary. One good thing is that it is not vital to get the fleece off in one piece, as it is with sheep.

When the fleece is removed from a goat it is 'skirted', meaning that all the less

A fine display of hand-crafted mohair garments.

CASHMERE GOATS

Although there is not a cashmere breed, there are quite a lot of goats throughout the world that are kept for cashmere production. Cashmere, like mohair, is secondary hair growing from secondary follicles. However, it is not the main coat, but grows as an insulating down under the main coat of primary hair.

Cashmere is the finest natural fibre known, and was the fibre used to manufacture the famous ring shawls brought back to the West by Marco Polo

some 700 years ago: these were so fine they could be drawn through a lady's wedding ring. The finest cashmere will be less than 10 microns in diameter, and as with mohair, white hair is the most valuable because it can be dyed any colour.

Cashmere is now produced throughout the Mongolian People's republic, Tibet, the Chinese People's Republic, Iran, Afghanistan and the Indian Himalayas. As some of these countries become more industrialized and process their own raw materials such as cashmere, the supply of material for processing in the West becomes limited, and alternative home supplies are considered.

The interest in cashmere production in the UK stems mainly from the use of goats for other purposes, such as the improvement of hill grazing for sheep. Goats are particularly good for this as they can graze out scrub, rushes and various grass-inhibiting weeds in environments where the use of machinery is not practicable.

Having established a use for goats, various workers have sought some form of direct income from the goats themselves. In the case of the hill grazing example, cashmere production is appropriate as it is likely that in this particular environment

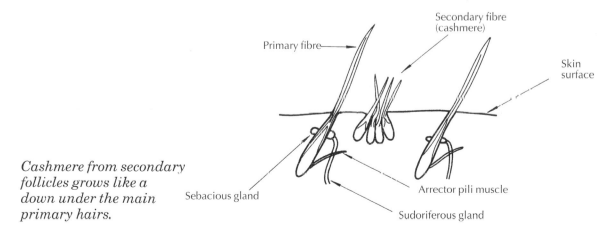

Cashmere from secondary follicles grows like a down under the main primary hairs.

the right type of goat should produce reasonable quantities of cashmere.

In many of the traditional cashmere-producing countries, 100–200g (3–6oz) will be harvested from each goat by combing, and by picking the moulted cashmere from bushes. In more industrialized countries, however, such as in the West where labour is expensive, such methods and yields would not be economic on a commercial scale. Efforts are being made to improve yields by selectively breeding goats, and some animals now produce more than 500g (17.6oz).

The technology exists for separating the cashmere down from the outer primary hair, and this means that shearing is an option for harvesting the fibre. However, this needs to be done before the spring moult, and so leaves the problem of shorn goats in cold and often wet environments. If they were housed immediately after shearing, this would increase production costs. Treatment with hormones to control moulting, and the use of protective coats, are other options that are being investigated.

If yields can be improved and the harvesting problems solved, cashmere goats may be an attractive proposition for hill farmers where, by their selective grazing, they would complement and improve sheep production.

As with all other types of goat production at the hobby level, there is the opportunity for those with only a few goats to process their own cashmere, and to spin it and craft it into clothing which, like those made from mohair, if well made would sell well in the right area. Cashmere is so fine that even as little as two per cent will enhance clothing material, and it is often blended with wool, silk and other fibres.

CASHGORA

During the period when Angora goats were first imported into the UK and some other European countries, and when the prices for breeding stock were very high, there was a lot of interest in cross-breeding to grade up to pure Angora. This cross-breeding created another fibre which was hailed by the textile industry as the first new natural fibre for over 100 years.

It was produced from first and second crosses where an Angora buck had been mated to a dairy-type female. The progeny from such a cross develop a coat of soft, fluffy hair which has some of the properties of both cashmere and mohair, and the name 'cashgora' was given to it to reflect its source. It is finer than mohair, but unlike cashmere has a little lustre, and it has been used to manufacture some very fine material which has been employed in the making of some wonderful coats and skirts. The companies making garments from fine natural fibre became quite excited about cashgora, but because it has never been produced in significant quantities, it has never advanced beyond the novelty stage, with just a small number of garments being produced.

KEY POINTS

- There are three types of goat fibre: mohair from Angora goats; cashmere, or under-down; and cashgora from first cross Angoras.
- There is a good demand for goat fibre, but it must be of the best quality.
- Angora goats are shorn twice a year.
- Most people with small numbers of fibre-producing goats derive some income by spinning it, and knitting or weaving.

8   Goats for Meat

Of the 500 million goats in the world, about 90 per cent will be kept for their meat. Most of these will be in the developing countries. In the West, goat meat is eaten in those countries where goats have been part of agricultural production for a long time; this does not include the UK where there are still many prejudices against the goat, and where the majority of the population would not consider eating goat meat at all. However, as travel around Europe becomes easier, more people are discovering goat – usually as kid meat – on restaurant menus, and little by little the interest in it grows.

Anyone with goats, however small the number, is going to produce kids, of which 50 per cent will be male. There are two choices with these: they can be destroyed at birth, or they can be reared for meat. What should not happen is that they are reared with no idea for their future – there are too many unwanted male goats that often end up in unsatisfactory environments.

THE CHARACTERISTICS OF GOAT MEAT

Unlike sheep, most breeds of goat do not lay down thick accumulations of fat on their bodies, even when well fed. The largest deposit of fat in a goat is in the abdomen, with comparatively little under the skin (subcutaneous) or in and around the mucles (intra muscular). This means that a typical goat carcase is very lean as compared with a lamb carcase of similar weight: even with relatively mature animals, pink muscle meat is seen with only a small covering of fat – although there are some breed differences, with Angoras and Boers showing a bit more carcase fat than the dairy breeds.

A Comparison of Lamb and Kid Carcases					
	muscle	bone	subcutaneous fat	intramuscular fat	kidney fat
21kg (46lb) lamb carcase	55	12	16	17	4.1
20kg (44lb) kid carcase (dairy breed)	55.9	15.4	6.7	14.3	8.1
20.5kg (45lb) kid carcase (Angora x British Saanen)	56	14.6	12.5	17	4.6

When kid and lamb carcases of similar weight are compared it will be found that in terms of the yield of lean meat the two will be very similar, but the lamb carcase will have more fat, and the kid carcase will have a greater ratio of bone to meat.

This has important implications when preparing goat meat for sale. It is generally considered preferable to bone out the middle part of the carcase – the loin and breast – because of the unfavourable amount of bone. The main joints such as the legs and shoulders can be presented in a more conventional way.

Meat scientists have shown that goat meat has a high ultimate pH in comparison to other meats, and this gives the meat its darker colour and a high water-holding capacity. This suggests that some of the boned meat may be more suitable for processing into sausages, burgers and pate.

BREEDS FOR MEAT

Although more goats are kept for meat than any other product, there is only one developed meat breed anywhere in the world, and that is the Boer goat from South Africa. Over the last forty years or so the South Africans have selectively bred the indigenous local goat to improve the carcase conformation, and now have goats that are quite unique in size, weight and conformation. A few Boer goats were imported into England almost twenty years ago, and there are now quite a number of cross-bred and pure-bred goats around the country.

Other breeds that would be worth considering for meat production would be the heavier type of Anglo Nubian and the Angora, especially some of the Australasian Angoras which may not have such good mohair, but which often have good bodyweight and conformation. If the market for goat meat improved, it is likely that Boers or other meat types would be used to mate young goats to produce first kids that would be suitable for rearing for meat. If Angora types are used it is possible that marketable cross-bred fibre such as cashgore may also be produced.

SELLING GOAT MEAT

As already discussed, there are real prejudices in the UK concerning eating goat meat. This situation has improved, but there is still an image problem and, apart from this poor image, they are more usually thought of as pet rather than as farm animals. Added to all this there is the problem of what to call the meat. We have venison for deer, beef for cattle, pork for pig and most sheep meat tends to be called lamb. In some other countries goat meat is called chevon, cabrita and chevrette, and it is possible that names like this would be more acceptable than just simply 'goat meat' or even 'kid meat'.

With a little local marketing and promotion it should be possible to sell profitably small numbers of kids as butchered meat direct to the end user. As already discussed, it has many attractive properties, and once it has been tried, it is likely that customers will want to purchase some more. There is also a great deal of scope for imaginative presentation and possibly added value by processing some of the boned meat into sausages, burgers and pate.

If goat meat is to be sold, the goats must be slaughtered in a licensed abattoir and the meat inspected and stamped as fit for human consumption. Sadly, new legislation regarding meat hygiene has brought about the demise of many small abattoirs where small numbers of goats could be dealt with in a more humane environment than they are in some of the larger, approved, production-line systems.

A British Saanen and an Angora-cross British Saanen kid showing the different conformation, and a fine growth of cashgora fibre on the cross-bred.

ECONOMICS OF GOAT MEAT

If goat meat is to be sold profitably, then obviously the price must be greater than the cost of production. Most small-scale goat keepers will not cost out their own labour, but will be satisfied with a small profit over the direct rearing costs. If the milk from the dams is required for sale or for home consumption, the kids will be reared on an artificial milk replacer. If kids are fed milk to around eight weeks of age, and then reared on for a further three months, their feed will cost between £20–£30 depending on the milk replacer that is used. A few other costs, such as bedding and veterinary care, could add another £3–£4 per goat. At five to six months of age they should reach a liveweight of around 35kg (77lb), which means a carcase weight of around 18kg (40lb). This gives some idea of the price that would need to be obtained to make rearing kids for meat profitable.

Rearing kids naturally with their mothers so they run out to pasture together may seem a more attractive option, but usually kids reared in this way do not grow well, probably because of early exposure to heavy parasite burdens. Therefore this cheaper system is at the expense of having to look after the kids for much longer before they reach a suitable weight for slaughter. A breakdown of the costs and possible income from goat meat is shown in Chapter 11.

KEY POINTS

- Goat meat is very lean, and is low in cholesterol.
- Boer goats are the only developed meat breed.
- There is not an established market for goat meat in the UK, but selling direct to local customers can often be profitable for relatively small quantities.
- Rearing kids from dairy goats artificially can be quite costly, and a good price would be necessary in order to make the sale of the meat profitable.

9 Health and Disease

The best person to help with problems of health in goats is a veterinarian, but realistically it has to be recognized that professional veterinary help is expensive, and there are many occasions when the owners of livestock can deal with health problems in their animals themselves. If goats are well looked after in the correct environment they should remain healthy, and there should not be much need for calling out the vet. Everyone with goats in the UK should persuade their vets to become members of the Goat Veterinary Society which will bring them into contact with those particularly interested in goats, and thus a lot of information can be shared on goat health and disease. A good veterinarian will be able to suggest a herd health plan – whatever the number of goats involved – for the whole year, and by following this plan, problems should be minimized.

A problem for all goat keepers is the fact that very few veterinary products are licensed for use with goats. This does not mean they will not work – in most cases, following the guidelines for sheep or cattle will be satisfactory for goats. However, if milk is being sold there will be problems because it must not be sold for consumption for a statutory seven days after the last treatment if unlicensed products are used.

Goats seem to have a low pain threshold, and do not tolerate ill health very well. This means there is much scope for the owner to give special attention to a sick goat in an effort to keep it feeding and taking an interest in life. With all ruminants, it is most important that they keep eating: once the rumen is starved of food the rumen micro-organisms will die, and it is very difficult to get the system working again. If a goat does stop eating, a wide variety of plants and tit-bits should be tried. Weed species such as dock and dandelion are often eaten when all else fails. Some tree leaves such as oak and ivy are often appreciated, as long as not too much is fed – many tree species are poisonous.

Giving a sub-cutaneous injection under the skin at the base of the neck.

FOOT CARE

Everyone who keeps goats will be faced with the problem of foot care sooner or later. The hooves of goats grow continuously, and unless they are on exceptionally hard, stony ground, they will need regular trimming. Angora goats originate from relatively dry environments, and they in particular seem to have a lot of foot problems when kept on grass.

It is recommended that feet should be trimmed at least every two months: if it is not done regularly, badly overgrown hooves can cause lameness, and even a permanently damaged foot. Regular trimming also means the goats will be regularly checked for foot-rot: although not a big problem with goats, this can sometimes cause very severe damage which can be avoided with early treatment.

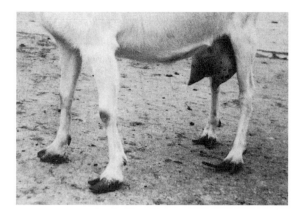

Feet that are badly over-grown can result in permanent deformities.

Trimming can be done with a sharp knife, or special foot-trimming clippers, or both. If possible, someone with experience should demonstrate the technique before a novice has a go. Until one is sure what to

A badly over-grown hoof.

Trimming feet with the goat tethered.

After trimming.

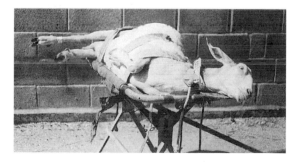

A turn-over crate for foot trimming.

do, it is better to trim off a little of the nail often, rather than a lot in one go.

The foot-rot bacteria thrives in warm, wet conditions such as a foot with mud or faeces trapped between the toes, or under an overgrown nail that creates a pocket usually filled with soil and faeces. Regular trimming will help avoid this problem, but if areas of infection are found, the nail around these should be trimmed to expose as much of the infected area as possible, and then the lesion treated with an antibiotic spray. Those containing oxytetracycline are particularly effective. The foot-rot bacteria does not survive long in the soil and if pastures are rested free of goats for three weeks this, along with treatment, will help eradicate the problem.

During wet weather goats sometimes get an infection between the toes that is commonly called scold. This is caused by the same foot rot bacteria and thus responds to the same antibiotics. It helps if, after treatment, the goat can be put onto a dry surface to allow the antibiotic spray to take effect, rather than be washed away as would be the case if the goat was on wet grass.

INTERNAL PARASITES

Internal parasites, often grouped under the generic name 'worms', are a particular problem in goats. It has been estimated that in any typical population of goats effective worm control would bring about a seventeen per cent increase in either growth rate or milk production.

All animals are infested with parasites, but many develop a degree of resistance and thus the parasite burden does not become so great that health is particularly affected. Sheep are an example of this, but goats are not. In fact goats do not seem to have much resistance at all, and thus internal parasites can be a major problem.

One explanation for this is that the sheep is an animal that grazes close to the ground, and by always ingesting parasite larvae, has evolved a degree of resistance to infestation. The goat, however, is a browser – that is to say, an animal that eats leaves of shrubs and trees at a higher level – and thus does not ingest many parasite larvae and as a result has not evolved with the same degree of resistance.

Goats that are kept on the same area of land for long periods are almost certain to build up heavy infestations which may or may not result in clinical signs. In bad cases they will have diarrhoea and will lose condition. Because internal parasite problems are so common, it is best to assume that this is the problem with any goat showing these signs, and to treat it with a worm drench (anthelmintic) immediately. If a faeces sample can be collected before treating the goat it will be possible, with the help of the vet, to have this analysed to see if parasites are the problem.

Broadly speaking there are three types of worm drench: the levamisoles, the benzamidazoles and the avamectins. Many of the levamisoles are no longer available; recent studies have shown that more and more parasites are showing resistance to the benzamidazoles; and most of the avamectins have a twenty-eight-day milk withdrawal period.

The problem of anthelmintic resistance has potentially serious consequences, and to avoid the problem getting even worse, regular treatment, at the correct dose level, is necessary, and together with the vet, a strategy for keeping the parasite burden as low as possible should be devised.

Most of these parasites have a very complicated life cycle involving several stages, and the period when levels of infestation rise are spring, mid-summer and early autumn. The spring rise is due to the goats ingesting over-wintered larvae, plus the rise in faecal eggs immediately after kidding. Goats that are housed all the year do not get the opportunity to ingest larvae, and in time will become more or less worm free.

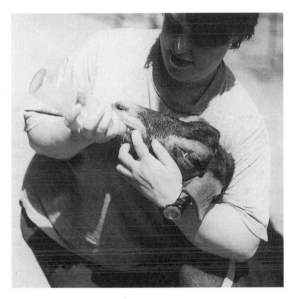

Giving a worm drench using a glass drink bottle.

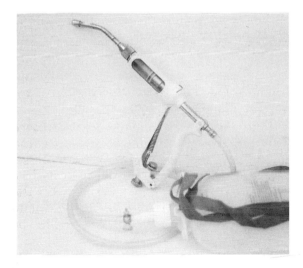

A drenching gun that can be adjusted to give a measured amount of worm drench.

Goats that remain in the same field or paddock for long periods are most at risk, as they will be exposed to high levels of larvae on the grass. To avoid this, paddocks would have to remain free of goats, sheep and deer for more than one year in order to break the parasites' life cycle.

EXTERNAL PARASITES

Lice and mange (caused by mites) can be a common problem in untreated goats. When goats are infested with lice they will spend a lot of time rubbing against fence posts, wire mesh and hurdles, and their coats can look rough and in poor condition. In extreme cases they will lose body condition and will look unwell. On close examination the lice can be seen with the naked eye, usually around the head and neck. They are about the size of a small hay seed, and move quite rapidly when exposed.

Mange occurs in various forms, and each type is caused by a different type of mite, all of which burrow into the skin. **Chorioptic mange** is quite common on goats, and appears as a diffuse reddening of the skin with extensive scabs, sometimes over quite a large area. The

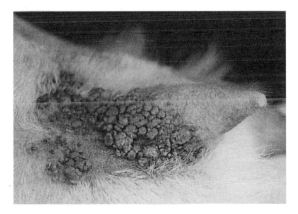

Scabs from chorioptic mange on a goat's udder.

mites burrow very deep into the skin, making them hard to find for making a positive diagnosis. **Demodectic mange** appears as local pustules, caused by the mite invading the hair follicles and the sebacious glands. **Sarcoptic mange** is usually seen as large areas of dry, flaky skin with a lot of irritation. If the infestation is bad the goats will lose condition and, as with all the other forms of mange, secondary infection of the skin, causing lesions, is always a possibility.

Unfortunately the number of products available to treat goats against these parasites is constantly reducing. Many products have been withdrawn because of possible damage to the environment, and most of those that *are* available involve milk withdrawal. Products containing selenium sulphide seem to be moderately effective for most types of mange. Again, because of constant changes, it is important to consult a veterinarian for advice regarding available treatments.

CLOSTRIDIAL DISEASES

The clostridial bacteria are a group of anaerobic bacteria that live in oxygen-free environments, and cause many diseases which are fatal through the effect of the powerful toxins these bacteria produce. Two clostridial diseases that affect man are botulism caused by *Clostridium botulinum*, and tetanus caused by *Clostridium tetani*. Clostridial bacteria live in the gut of most ruminants where normally they do not cause any problems. However, there are times when they proliferate, and the toxins they produce prove fatal.

The clostridial diseases most commonly seen in goats, caused by *Clostridium perfringens* type D, are enterotoxaemia in adults, and pulpy kidney disease in kids. In both cases they are usually seen after an abrupt change in diet, when for a short period the digestion of feedstuffs may be incomplete, and conditions in the gut encourage the bacteria to multiply. This may occur when goats are turned out to pasture after being over-wintered indoors, or when they are moved to a new environment – for instance, when they are bought by a new owner. Clostridial diseases should be suspected where goats become ill and die very rapidly, especially if this is associated with some diarrhoea.

It is possible to vaccinate against clostridial diseases. The current observation by the Goat Veterinary Society is that many of the vaccines that cover a wide range of clostridial types are not so effective, so they recommend using one that is specific for the clostridial types that are a problem in goats. Adult goats should be vaccinated twice a year, not once as with sheep, and if one of these is during late pregnancy, some immunity will be passed on to the kids. Kids from vaccinated mothers should be vaccinated at 8 weeks of age, and those from unvaccinated mothers at 3–4 weeks of age. In both cases they should be given a booster vaccination 4–6 weeks later.

LISTERIOSIS

This disease is caused by the soil-borne bacteria *Listeria monocytogenes*. It can occur almost anywhere, and can contaminate anything that has been in contact with soil. Goats are particularly susceptible, and most commonly become infected from silage. Maize or grass silage can be a problem, and even when well made in a clamp, it would appear that the listeria bacteria can thrive. This is presumably because parts of the clamp have not fermented so well, and have therefore not reached the level of acidity that inhibits the bacteria. Bagged or baled silage is a much greater risk than clamp silage.

A goat showing the early stages of listeriosis with its head tilted to one side.

The most common sign of the disease is when a goat holds its head slightly to one side, usually with one ear hanging down. As the disease progresses the mouth will be held open, the tongue may hang out, and a lot of saliva will be seen; by this stage the goat will have lost the ability to swallow, and so will not be able to eat or drink.

Treatment is rarely successful because severe brain damage will have occurred by the time symptoms are seen. There are, however, reports of cases recovering when treated with antibiotics very early on. It may be practicable in a small herd to identify early cases by taking body temperatures; then if any goat with an elevated temperature is treated with high doses of antibiotic intravenously, it may be possible to stop the progress of the disease. Obviously this must be done with the help of a veterinarian.

Listeriosis can cause abortion, and it may also infect the eyes, particularly in young goats or kids. It must also be remembered that it is transmissable to humans (zoonotic), and it would therefore be unwise to consume unpasteurized milk from herds with cases of this disease.

MASTITIS

Infections of the udder are much less common in goats than in cows. It is likely that because the udder of a goat is rarely dirty it is not under such a great challenge from infective bacteria. However, most of the bacteria that cause this problem in cows can infect goats if conditions are suitable. The udder is most at risk of infection during and immediately after milking, and when kids are being suckled. The risks after milking can be minimized by dipping or spraying the teats with an approved bacteriacidal teat dip as soon as milking has finished.

The first signs of mastitis are clots appearing in the milk. As the infection progresses blood may appear, and the milk may become lumpy, discoloured and smelly. In bad cases the goat will be generally unwell, with an elevated temperature. It is important to initiate treatment as soon as possible. If the infection is confined to the udder, squeezing antibiotic cream into the udder via the teat canal for three days may cure the condition; a fresh tube of intra-mammary antibiotic should be used for each half of the udder. If the goat is ill, however, injected antibiotics may be necessary.

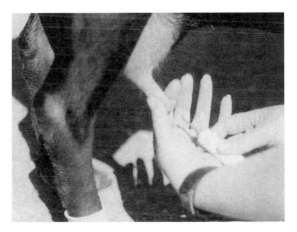

Treating mastitis with an intra-mammary antibiotic cream.

In cases of toxic mastitis the udder or part of the udder may go black within a few hours, and after some weeks may slough off. The goat may be ill, in which case again, injected antibiotics will be necessary. On the other hand sometimes, in spite of a smelly infected udder, the goat may not be ill at all, and even though she may lose half of her udder, she will make a complete recovery.

JOHNE'S DISEASE

Johne's disease – otherwise known as 'paratuberculosis' – is caused by the bacteria *Mycobacterium avium subspp paratuberculosis*, and has the potential to infect most ruminant species. It appears to be quite prevalent in goats, though clinical disease is often only seen in larger groups, probably initiated by low levels of stress. Typical symptoms are a few days of diarrhoea followed by a fairly rapid loss of condition, and if milking, a rapid decline in milk yield with the goat drying off in two to three weeks.

If the disease is left to run its course the goat will become very emaciated, and will not be able to compete with others. Death usually occurs within two to three months from the time the first symptoms were observed.

There is no treatment for this disease, and in fact it is best to remove suspected cases as soon as they are observed because they will be shedding the bacteria in their faeces and thus will be a danger to other goats. It is possible to test blood and faeces for the presence of the bacteria, but neither test is completely reliable. It is also possible to carry out a skin reaction test, as with tuberculosis, but again it is possible to get false negatives.

There is no cure for Johne's Disease, but a vaccine is available which must be given within one month of birth. It is not completely effective, but the incidence of the clinical disease will be considerably reduced in herds with this problem as long as all kids are vaccinated, and all goats showing symptoms of the disease are removed. Anyone starting up a new herd of goats should consider buying only vaccinated stock because of the high risk of buying in this disease.

DISEASES CAUSING ABORTION

There are a number of diseases that will cause pregnant goats to abort. The most likely will be enzootic abortion (chlamydia); toxoplasmosis; listeriosis; campylobacter (vibriosis); and Q fever. Most of these are transmissable to humans (zoonotic) and are a particular risk to pregnant women. It is important to enlist the help of a vet and send aborted foetuses and placenta to a veterinary investigation laboratory in order to obtain a positive diagnosis; an appropriate course of action can then be taken.

CAPRINE ARTHRITIS AND ENCEPHALITIS (CAE)

This disease is caused by a lentivirus closely related to the one that causes maedi-visna in sheep. It is a major problem in some European countries and in the USA and Australia, and in some of these countries about 80 per cent of the goats will react positively to the blood test for the virus. In the UK there is an accreditation scheme, and a large number of goat keepers have been testing their animals for almost twenty years. It is estimated that no more than 2 per cent of the UK goat population would be positive reactors.

The signs of the disease are varied. Mature goats may develop arthritis and find walking painful. The knee joints may be inflamed and swollen, and the goats will slowly lose condition; in extreme cases they will become so weak they will hardly be able to stand. There is no cure for this disease, and if a high incidence is to be avoided it is most important that goats are regularly tested, and any animals testing positive culled.

SCRAPIE

This disease, like CAE, is probably more important politically than as a major disease problem, because the fact that it does exist in the UK, mainly in sheep, makes the export of goats out of the country more difficult. In fact the incidence in the UK goat population is very low, and most people keeping goats will never see it.

Scrapie has a long incubation period, and is rarely seen in goats less than two years old. A goat with scrapie may scratch and nibble at its skin, particularly when touched; it may also show signs of inco-ordination, tremors, salivation and jerky movement of the eyes.

There is no cure for scrapie, and it is also a notifiable disease. The British Government is currently discussing an eradication scheme to remove the risk from all sheep and goats in the country.

METABOLIC DISEASES

Sometimes a goat can become ill, not because of any infectious agent, but because the body system is not working correctly and is not metabolizing in a normal manner. A classical case of this is during pregnancy. The ruminant digestive system takes up a lot of room, and the rumen in particular is a very large organ which has to digest large quantities of plant material. A pregnant goat may be carrying three, or even sometimes four developing foetuses which also take up a lot of the abdominal space; and if she is in very good condition she may well have a quite large deposit of fat in the abdomen, too. As a result she may be reduced to taking in relatively small meals, and so it is important that her diet at this time is adequate and balanced.

If it is not, it may mean that she finds herself short of energy, in which case she may start to metabolize her own body fat; and if she does, chemicals called 'ketone bodies' are formed, and these may poison her system, giving rise to the condition called 'ketosis' or 'acetonaemia'. In sheep this often occurs as 'twin lamb disease' or 'pregnancy toxaemia'; in goats it is more typically seen as a post kidding acetonaemia.

A goat suffering from this condition will appear listless, with loss of appetite, and her breath will smell of acetone (pear drops). It is a difficult condition to treat, but an injection of corticosteroids and a multi-vitamin preparation may restore correct metabolism in about 30 per cent of cases. Diagnostic sticks are available for testing body fluids for the presence of ketone bodies. This is very much a situation where preventive treatment is preferable to a cure, and goat keepers should appreciate just how important it is that the goat does obtain enough energy from her diet during late pregnancy; with this in mind, her rations should be spread over four feeds a day.

There are many other diseases that can occur in goats, but some of the most common have been described in this chapter. It is important that a good relationship with a veterinarian is developed so that together the best course of action is taken when health problems occur. If they are not members already, all veterinarians with goat clients should be encouraged to join the Goat Veterinary Society.

NOTIFIABLE DISEASES

In the event of an outbreak of certain specific diseases in farm livestock, the police or local government veterinary department must be notified. These include anthrax; bovine tuberculosis; brucellosis; foot and mouth disease; scrapie.

ZOONOTIC DISEASES

Certain diseases are transmissable from animals to humans, and it is good policy to assume that any animal can carry potentially harmful micro-organisms. Practices that observe methods of good hygiene should therefore be followed at all times. Zoonotic diseases include anthrax; brucellosis; enzootic abortion; leptospirosis; listeriosis; orf; ringworm; toxoplasmosis.

The most vulnerable are the young and the elderly, and people in these categories should not be exposed to undue risks. Drinking unpasteurized milk could be considered as an unacceptable risk, and it is important that children in particular should wash their hands thoroughly after handling goats, or indeed any animals.

KEY POINTS

- Goats are normally healthy animals, and with good husbandry should not incur large vet bills.
- Feet need regular trimming, although foot rot is not usually a major problem.
- Internal parasites are a major problem with all goats that are grazing outside.
- Take care to ascertain the health status of goats for sale before agreeing to buy.
- Some diseases are transmissable to humans, and this should be born in mind when drinking unpasteurized milk.
- Mastitis should not be a problem as long as practices of good hygiene are followed at milking.

10 Showing

By Hilary Matthews

Showing can be great fun and very rewarding, but it will not appeal to everyone. Always remember the words of the great British Alpine breeder, Mrs Arthur Abbey, who many years ago said that: 'Different judges have different ideals, and for this reason different animals win.' These are sensible words to remember in success, and a great comfort in defeat.

Showing goats in the UK falls into three main categories:

- Day shows for all ages of females where judging is done on conformation only;
- Male and youngstock shows where again, judging is purely on conformation;
- Inspection classes for adult females incorporating a 24-hour milking trial, coupled with all ages of female youngstock.

The last-mentioned type of showing is often associated with the bigger agricultural shows, and always involves at least one night away from home; in the case of the larger shows – for example, the Royal Show – you may be away for at least four nights. This type of showing, where the inspection classes are governed by the amount of milk the goats give, although not unique, is not common throughout the rest of the world. However, it is an excellent way of showing a female goat's true worth, and has always given British goats a very good reputation world-wide.

Generally, the milking goats need to be on the showground at the end of the afternoon prior to the show (youngstock are often allowed in on the morning of the show). The goat is then milked by her owner, and by a given time (say, 18.30hr) the goat is checked to be empty (stripped) by a steward. The goat is then not allowed to leave her pen until milking time the following morning.

For the adult female goat there are two separate classes: the milking classes and the inspection classes. If the goat is entered in an inspection class as well as a milking class, then she is allowed into the ring for udder inspection prior to milking; here, in classes determined according to the goat's breed, the judge handles and examines the full udder. Once these classes are finished, milking takes place under strict rules, with the goats being milked out by a set time (say, 08.30hr). Each goat's milk is weighed, and a sample is taken to be tested for butterfat and protein content. After breakfast, judging begins again (usually around 10.00hr) for those goats entered for both the milking and inspection classes. The milking-only goats remain in their pens.

The judge now examines the goats (still in their relevant classes). The judge has, you will remember, already seen them with a full udder, and now will examine the empty udder and give full consideration to their conformation. He/she will have a book in which will be noted the goat's age, the date she kidded, and how much milk she gave at the morning

The line-up being scrutinized by the judge.

The judge examining a goat in the line.

milking trial; this will be taken into consideration when making the final placing. If the prettiest goat in the class has given hardly any milk, then she should not be considered for the top placings unless the standard of the goats forward is very poor.

Each class is placed from first to last, and at the completion of the breed judging the top four goats – this number could rise to six if the judge deemed the class to be of a very high standard – from each breed are asked to come forward for the judge's final consideration.

At this stage milk becomes a significant factor, and the judge will select the best goat, followed by his/her second, then third choice, and so on down to the very last goat present. This is called an 'inspection production line-up'. The goat at the top of the line, if the judge considers her worthy enough, and of championship potential, is awarded a challenge certificate, and the second-placed goat a reserve challenge cert-ificate. The remaining first- and second-placed goats from the breed classes may be awarded breed challenge certificates, and reserve breed challenge certificates if the judge thinks they are of a suitable standard eventually to become breed champions.

The top goat is awarded as many points as there are goats put forward, the reserve goat one less point, and so on down to the bottom-placed goat which is awarded just one point. These points will be added to the milking competition points, and the goat gaining the most points overall will be awarded an inspection production

BGS Female Champion

This is a female goat that has won three challenge certificates under three different judges, and must have gained no fewer than eighteen points in a milking competition at the same shows. She must also have won three inspection production challenge certificates, with a minimum of eighteen milking competition points. She must also qualify for a Q star (Q*).

BGS Female Breed Champion

This is a female goat that has won five breed challenge certificates under three different judges. She must also have gained no fewer than sixteen points in the milking competitions at the same shows, and also qualified for a star (*) or Q star (Q*).

challenge certificate which will go towards the goat becoming an eventual champion.

Judging then continues with the rest of the youngstock, and is done purely on conformation. From the goatling section the judge will eventually select the Best and Reserve Best Goatling, and similarly from the kid section, the Best and the Reserve Best Kid. These will come forward against the Best and the Reserve Best Milker for the Best in Show. Almost inevitably, and quite rightly, this will be awarded to the mature milking animals.

This is not the end of the story though, and by 18.30hr (this will depend on the time the goats were stripped out the night before) all the goats in the milking trial must be milked out and, like the morning session, the milk weighed and sampled again. The samples are then sent for analysis, and when the results are obtained (often a number of days after the show) a formula involving the weight of milk, butterfat and protein percentage, and length of time since kidding, is used to obtain total points for each goat. Points can range from forty plus in very exceptional circumstances, down to single figures.

But now – and here comes the twist in the tail – the goat that was awarded the challenge certificate must get at least eighteen points, whilst the breed challenge certificate goats must obtain at least sixteen points. If the goat does not do this, then the reserve goat, providing she has obtained the necessary points, will take either the challenge certificate or the breed challenge certificate.

As the milking trial is also run on a class basis, the goats who stayed in their pen (perhaps not the prettiest of ladies) may stand a very good chance of winning. Awards are also given for butterfat percentage, in the form of a Q star (Q*) and star (*) affix (see also Chapter 1). These awards stay with the goat all her life and are handed down, in part, to her offspring and to their offspring.

How to Gain a BGS* or Q* Affix Star (*)

This is gained when eighteen points are obtained in a BGS-recognized milking competition, subject to the butterfat percentage being at least 3.25 per cent at each milking.

Q Star (Q*)

This is when twenty points are obtained in a BGS-recognized milking competition, subject to the butterfat percentage being at least 4 per cent at each milking, and the total yield for the competition being

(i) not less than 4.5kg (9.9lb) when a goat has kidded for less than 365 days; and
(ii) not less then 4kg (8.8lb) when a goat has kidded for 365 days or more.

The female progeny of a goat that has qualified for a star or a Q star are eligible, upon themselves qualifying for either of these awards, for the appropriate affix, which should be followed by a numeral indicating the number of ancestors in the direct female line that have qualified for either the star or Q star: thus a goat bearing the affix Q*3 will itself have qualified for the Q star, and its dam, grand-dam and great grand-dam will have qualified for either the star or Q star, whilst the affix *2 will denote that the goat itself will have qualified for the star, and its dam and grand-dam have qualified for either the star or the Q star.

Outside factors can greatly affect the goat's milk at the show: for example, a very bad journey, unpalatable or just different drinking water, and the temperature, particularly extreme heat, can reduce both the milk yield and the butterfat percentage. The protein content, luckily, generally remains unaffected. A great deal of skill is required to combat outside and environmental factors, and to get the goats to milk as they would at home, and the whole experience proves a great challenge.

The other two categories of show – male shows and day shows – are judged on the looks of the goats only, and although they are generally fun, are not as important an aid to goat breeding and selection as are the female milking shows. Males may become champions and breed champions if they are awarded three challenge certificates and four breed challenge certificates respectively, but to stop infertile males having any chance of lasting honours, before the goat is given the title of 'champion' or 'breed champion', he must have produced a number of milk-recorded daughters, or daughters who have been awarded stars * or Q stars at shows.

SOME THOUGHTS ON THE FIRST SHOW

As already mentioned at the beginning, showing is not for everyone, but if you decide to give it a go, then we should consider a few 'do's' and 'don'ts'. First of all, make sure that your animals are in good condition – no amount of washing or skill at showing will disguise a thin goat in poor bodily condition. Some goats are natural show goats and have what can now be called the 'wow' factor: these animals, right from the kid stage, are really at home in the ring – their ears and tails come up, they are alert, are obviously enjoying themselves, and naturally draw the judge's eye to them.

Others merely put up with the showing, and need to be shown with great skill to get the best out of them. So try and look at your goats objectively at home, and pick out not only the best ones, but also the most forward and showy ones, even if they do have faults. There are very few things more embarrassing for both the

---

BGS Male Champion

This is a male goat that has won three challenge certificates under three different judges. He must also have sired three daughters who have qualified for any combination of the following awards as defined by the BGS:

Star (*), Q Star (Q*);
C, R, RM or AR (milk recording awards).

BGS Male Breed Champion

This is a male goat that has won four breed challenge certificates under three different judges. He must also have sired a daughter who has qualified for one of the following awards as defined by the BGS:

Star (*), Q Star (Q*);
C, R, RM or AR (milk recording awards).

The responsibility for claiming the male awards is with the owner or breeder, who must forward the necessary information to the BGS secretary.

---

experienced and the novice exhibitor than trying to drag and cajole a goat, which steadfastly refuses to walk, around the ring. Neither the goat nor the exhibitor enjoys this, and a bit of ring training at home can prove priceless.

Persuade someone whose opinion you value, to look at each goat with you and assess its strengths and weaknesses – providing you are aware of them, some faults can be improved by good ringcraft. If you have to evaluate your own goats without assistance, to find out the best way to stand that particular animal, use a full-length mirror in the garden and practise holding the goat in front of it.

For the first show, attend the local goat club's day show, which will often consist of just goatling and kid classes. Most clubs also offer an earmarking service which is often carried out at the show – so you can kill two birds with one stone by entering a class and having your kid tattooed as well. Remember though, never have your goat tattooed before the class – black tattoo paste, white coats and especially white kids do *not* go well together!

For every show you enter, make sure that you read the schedule carefully and enter your goat in the right class – even the most experienced exhibitors have been known to enter the wrong class – and make a note of the date. Always enter the show in plenty of time – even in this computer-orientated society, there is nothing more annoying for the hard-working show secretary than late entries. Almost all shows require a CAE certificate to be presented either with your entry form or when you arrive at the show, so make sure you get your goats blood-tested in good time.

Pack up your vehicle and trailer the night before a show, and make sure that you allow yourself plenty of time for travelling. Make sure all hoof trimming is done well in advance of the show, and always wash your goat the day before as the judge will not appreciate being presented with a slightly damp, fuzzy specimen.

If you are at an overnight show you may prefer to wash your goat at the show, in case it gets dirty whilst travelling. And if you have coloured goats, it does not mean you do not have to wash them: whilst examining an animal the judge will be able to feel the dirt in its coat even if it is not obvious to the naked eye, and it is annoying if, as a judge, you have to interrupt your concentration to keep washing your hands between goats, simply to remove the dirt. White goat owners here deserve every sympathy – a lick and a promise simply will not do, and they must be washed before every show.

WASHING PROCEDURE

There are many ways of washing goats, and providing you generally stick to the same routine and use your common sense, then your goats will come to no harm. Cold water can be used, but warm is appreciated by the goats on colder days and at the start of the show season when a longer, more thorough wash is required.

There are many types of shampoo and coat glosses on the market, and the final decision rests on personal choice and recommendations by experienced goat keepers. Remember to get everything ready – buckets, towels, goat coats, brushes and so on – before bringing your goat out, as she will not appreciate standing there while you try to get everything gathered together. Always use a nylon collar when washing, as the colour in leather ones will run and stain the goat.

Fill one bucket with soapy water, and another larger bucket with clean rinsing water. Sponge the goat all over with soapy water, remembering to include the head in your bathing routine – your goat will soon get used to it. For more persistent stains on the flanks, use 'Windsor white' soap scrubbed directly onto the stain with a brush. Rinse the goat well all over, and remove the surplus water with a waterbrush; then dry the goat briskly with a clean towel until she is almost dry. Make sure you dry her ears and udder well. At this stage it is advisable to apply a coat gloss by way of a spray applicator: rub this well into the coat by hand, and then, with the waterbrush, lay the coat down flat and towards its natural direction.

The goat should then have its properly fitted coat put on. If it is a cold day, the coat should be removed and a dry one put in its place after about half an hour. Providing the coat is well fitting and not causing the goat any distress, then it should not be removed until the goat enters the ring, and it should be replaced the moment the goat gets back into her pen. The coat only comes off at the end of the showing classes. It is best to have a number of coats in a variety of materials ranging from heavyweight towelling to light cotton, so that all weather conditions can be catered for.

EXHIBITOR'S DRESS

All goat shows expect exhibitors to wear white coats while showing their goats, though white boiler suits are acceptable for showing male goats. A tidy appearance on the part of the exhibitor helps to show the goat off to its full potential, and something like shorts and trainers are really not acceptable, especially at County Show level.

If you have taken a great deal of time to present your animal to the best of your ability, then five minutes preparing yourself is time well spent. This is particularly relevant for the 'inspection classes' after breakfast when the public are present; however, it is not quite so important for udder inspection.

EQUIPMENT

For your first overnight show make sure you prepare a checklist: it will assuredly prove invaluable, and can be used for future shows. Divide the list into sections, as follows:

Goat Equipment

This should include such things as hayracks, troughs, water buckets, milking buckets, kid feeding bottles, pen screens, goat coats and towels, washing equipment, show box (including grooming equipment, collars and leads and so on), and a goat first-aid kit.

Goat Feed

This should include hay, straw (not all shows provide straw), greens, branches, concentrates, Alfa A, sugar beet, mineral licks, a supply of milk for your kids (it is a British Goat Society ruling that milk produced during the milking competion should not be used for kid feeding), and so on.

Human Requirements

These include a white showing coat, bedding, cooking utensils and eating implements, a gas bottle, picnic table and chairs, food and drink, torches, clock, plenty of changes of clothing, wellingtons, medication, hot water bottle, schedule, entry tickets and so on.

Almost all of the above items are essential for an overnight show, but your list will include many other items as well.

ON ARRIVAL AT THE OVERNIGHT SHOW

Always arrive with plenty of time to spare, as neither you or your goat will appreciate the stress that goes with trying to unload in a hurry. Firstly, on arrival, park your vehicle as close to the goat tent as you can, and if possible, open the door of your trailer and all the windows in your van to let in some air. Then go and locate the steward or secretary who will show you to your pens. Strawing up the pens can be done at a later stage, so initially work out which goat is going in which pen. Only then unload the goats. Watering them should be one of your first priorities, followed by feeding them hay. Concentrates should not be fed for an hour or so after travelling. Always try to keep to the same feeding routines as at home, and never introduce a new concentrate feed.

Remember to pack a sandwich and a drink for yourself so that you can stop after unloading the goats, and have a quick drink and a bite to eat. It is easy to become dehydrated on a hot day after a long journey, coupled with the hard work of unloading. A lot of shows provide a 'kitchen tent' where all your food, cooking utensils, and a chair and table can be placed – although these should always be sorted out after you have seen to your goats.

Later in the afternoon, after the goats have settled in, the bathing can be carried out, and beard and chest hair and so on removed or tidied up. After bathing, make sure you sort out your lapel numbers, and the collars and leads for the morning – thin rolled collars and small unobtrusive leads are generally considered the best. Always put your labels with your goat's name and number – which the show will provide – on the milking buckets, and make sure these are handed to the stewards at the correct time.

Don't forget to make your bed up. If you do not have a caravan you could be sleeping in your van, trailer or in the goat tent, and there is nothing worse than wanting to go to bed but suddenly remembering you have done everything else except for preparing your own bed!

ON THE DAY OF SHOWING

First, always make sure your goats are taken to the ring in as clean and near-perfect condition as you can manage. A clean white showing coat and tidy appearance on the part of the exhibitor all go a long way to enhancing the final effect that the judge sees.

Always be on time for your classes, as the judge will not appreciate being kept waiting; and always concentrate on your goat the whole time you are in the ring – which means not chatting to fellow

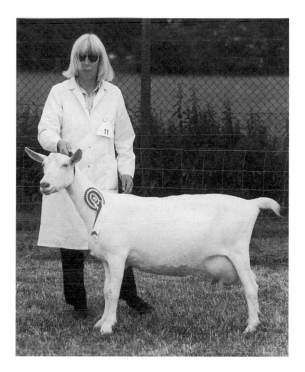

Hilary Matthews with Breed Champion Toddbrook Marrakesh.

exhibitors during the class! Even the very nicest of goats can become very ordinary if their owner loses concentration and does not show them to the best of their ability. Watch other classes and observe the top exhibitors and the techniques they employ to get the best out of their goats.

Above all, accept with dignity the judge's comments – after all, it is only an opinion – whatever your own opinion of him or her; and under no circumstances answer back.

Miss Jean Mostyn-Owen, a legend in her lifetime during sixty-five years of showing top quality goats, always said that the three most important words in relation to goat keeping and success in the show ring were 'attention to detail'. This is still true, and if you remember these words, and accept that different judges have different opinions, and learn from each show you attend, then success will come to you.

Showing is fun.

Finally, showing is fun, it is a great leveller, and not least, a wonderful way of making life-long friends throughout the country. Try it and see!

KEY POINTS

- Showing can be fun.
- Some show classes are judged on conformation alone, and some incorporate a milking trial.
- Many of the larger shows, especially if they include a milking trial, will involve at least one night away.
- The British Goat Society sets the rules for showing dairy goats, and the British Angora Goat Society for Angora goats.
- Most shows will only allow goats that are accredited or tested to be negative for the CAE virus to be shown.
- At shows, the appearance of the handler is almost as important as that of the goat.
- Attention to detail is most important.

11 Profitable Goat Keeping

Farming goats as a major source of income is outside the scope of this book. However, there are many ways in which goat keepers can make their hobby cost-effective, and by doing so may find that it pays for itself, or even makes a small profit. But before anyone commits themselves to goat keeping in the expectation that it will be profitable, there are a few points they should consider before they go too far.

With the current value of goat products, it is not possible to derive a full income from goats unless really large numbers are kept. With dairy goats the accepted rule is that it is not possible to produce a reasonable income from bulk milk production with less than 300 milking goats. If value is added to the milk by processing it, this number could be halved, but only if a particularly good product is made and good markets are developed for it.

With fibre goats even greater numbers would need to be kept if the raw fibre was going to be the principle product. Again, a reasonable income could possibly be achieved if the fibre from a large number of goats were processed and crafted into finished products for which good market outlets were developed.

The problem with any goat enterprise is that the profit per goat will not be very large, and therefore a reasonable number must be kept. And if large numbers are kept, a great deal of capital is required to buy the goats and set up the necessary infrastructure in the first place, and also annual overhead costs will be such that numbers will have to be maximized to reduce the cost per goat. Using milk production as an example, it costs almost as much to set up and run a milking unit for 100 goats as it does one for 400 goats; about the only difference will be the feed bill. And if milk is to be processed, the equipment necessary to produce dairy products of the quality that is now demanded is expensive, and these costs can only be justified if the throughput of milk is large enough.

Many of those who will read this book will have no intention of becoming large scale, profitable goat farmers. Nevertheless, this chapter will give them some guidance on how to allay the cost of keeping their goats by increasing the income that can be derived from them.

DAIRY GOATS

In the United Kingdom it is now necessary to register as a milk producer, under the Dairy Products (Hygiene) Regulations 1995, if the intention is to sell milk which will be used for human consumption. The main requirements for this are described in Chapter 7. It is these regulations that have brought about the demise of many small-scale goat milk producers because they found their premises did not comply with the regulations and that it would be too expensive to change them so that they would. However, anyone starting off in goat keeping should be able to create a milking environment that would comply with these regulations without too much extra cost.

In the first table below the cost of keeping a milking goat is shown, and this is compared in the second table that follows it with the income that may be derived from the milk produced by both a low- and a high-yielding goat.

Goat Milk Production Costs	
	£
Concentrate feed	60
Forage	40–20*
Straw	15
Vet and medicines	25
Dairy chemicals	5
Electricity/heating	5
Total	150–130*

*The forage cost will depend on whether or not the goat is grazing. The higher figure is for a housed goat.

The costs shown are realistic. The veterinary costs are high and are a good example of economy of scale. One goat would have to carry the whole cost of a visit from the vet, whereas in a large herd this would be spread over a large number of animals. If goats go out to graze there is a saving on forage cost, but during the winter they will need hay or some other conserved crop which will incur costs even if it is home grown. The total feed bill is an area where savings can be made, particularly with only a few goats, because garden and kitchen waste can supplement the ration and thus save money on bought-in feeds.

To produce some financial return from the goat or goats requires a very single-minded approach to cutting down on unnecessary expenditure, and successfully marketing whatever products are produced. It is unlikely that anyone with less than fifty milking goats would find a bulk outlet for their milk, and in fact it is unlikely that any dairy buying goat milk in bulk would be interested in collecting from anyone with fewer than 100 milking goats. It is possible that some specialist cheese makers may be interested in smaller quantities of milk, but it would only be a viable proposition to supply them if they were relatively close by. To give some idea of the possible financial return that could be achieved if outlets for the milk can be found or developed, the following table shows the return from both low- and high-yielding goats, and for both bulk and retail sales of packaged and pasteurized milk.

The Income From the Sale of Goat's Milk		
	Low yielder	High yielder
Annual milk yield (litres)	700	1,200
Milk value (in bulk)	£280	£480
Retail milk value (pasteurized/ in cartons)	£840	£1,440
Cost of packaging	£56	£96

The comparison between the costs and the retail value of the milk looks attractive at first, but it is important to realize that a large investment in equipment would be necessary to process milk for drinking. A small pasteurizer and a small carton-filling and sealing machine together would cost in excess of £10,000. At one time it was possible to process milk in this way with very basic facilities, but the new hygiene regulations mean this is no longer the case. In addition to the hygiene aspect, the market demands are such that only very professionally presented products are now acceptable, and thus packaging and presentation has become more expensive. This all means it is difficult for small producers to compete in this type of market unless they are able to invest a large amount of money.

An area where some relatively small producers are successful is in the speciality cheese market. Although it is just as necessary to have very high standards of production, the increase in value of the milk by using it for the manufacture of cheese can often compensate for the high cost of production. There are quite a number of people who have managed to break into this niche market and, once their cheese

became well known, have found the main constraint is the amount they are able to make.

In all of these small enterprises, if the owners were to cost their own time correctly, the income derived from this sort of activity would not compare well with many other more conventional occupations, especially considering the uncivilized hours it is necessary to work to milk the goats, to make the cheese, and to get it to the shops at the required time.

FIBRE GOATS

A very similar situation occurs with goat kept for their fibre, except that here the return is much less per animal – but then so is the work required to produce the fibre. With dairy goats it is a case of high cost and high returns per animal, whereas in the case of fibre, relatively low returns

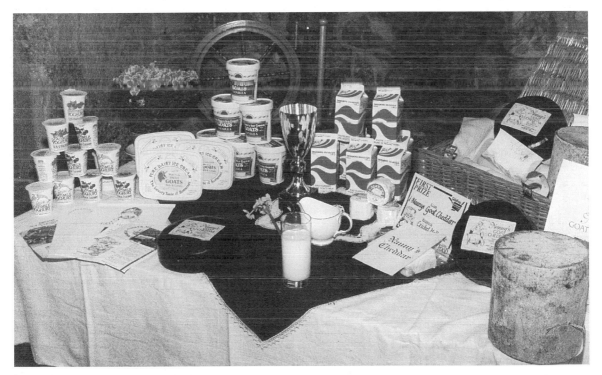

A display of British goat products.

The Costs Involved in Mohair Production	
	£
Concentrates	15
Forage	8
Straw	2
Vet & med	8
Shearing	3
Miscellaneous	2
Total	38

are achieved but are balanced against a lower cost of production.

Each case will be different, and these costs could vary. For example, vet fees could be higher, shearing may be carried out by the owner, and forage may be grown for slightly less cost. Moreover the income derived from Angora goats will depend on many factors, such as the yield and the quality of the mohair, whether value is added by processing, and whether garments are sold through a wholesaler or direct to the end user. The figures shown in the next table are typical of what would be currently achieved if the mohair was sold in its raw state. Also the income from selling weaned kids will depend on

The Income From an Angora Goat	
	£
Value of adult clip	12.5
Value of kid clip	22.0
Sale of kids	90.0
Sale of culls	3.0
Total	127.5

demand, and the quality of the kids; the figures shown are typical of what was being achieved at the time of writing.

A similar picture would be shown for cashmere production, the main difference being that, because the demand for cashmere is usually greater than the supply, the price tends to be more stable.

GOATS FOR MEAT

Generally speaking the market for goat meat in the UK is not good. However, because it is such a good product there is scope for producers to do some innovative marketing, and it is quite possible for someone producing just a few surplus kids each year to make a good profit. Exactly how much will depend very much on the cost of rearing: goat milk is an expensive feed for kids if it can be sold for a good price, and so it is often cheaper to rear them on a milk replacer. The cheapest rearing system of all is to leave kids with their mothers and to have them all grazing outside. However, as has already been discussed, goats, and kids in particular, are very susceptible to internal parasites, and this, and the fact that kids use up a lot of energy playing when outside, usually results in very poor growth rates. It is generally accepted that if kids are to grow well they should be kept indoors, or at least in covered yards.

The accompanying table compares the cost of three rearing methods with the returns from selling the meat directly to the consumer or wholesale to a butcher. It can be seen that rearing kids with their mothers outside gives the best profit, but this may take much longer because of slow growth rates. Also it would not be an option if the mothers were being kept for their milk.

As with all other goat products, there are opportunities to add value to goat meat by processing it. As discussed in

The Income From Meat Kids Using Three Different Rearing Methods			
(all units in pounds)			
	Butcher		**Retail**
30kg (66lb) kid value	30		40
Skin value	5		6
	35		46

Method *	A	B	C
Rearing costs	29	40	12
Slaughter and butchering costs	14	14	14

	A	B	C		A	B	C
Net profit	−12	−19	9		−3	−8	20

* Rearing methods

A Rationed milk replacer, weaned at 8 weeks.

B Ad lib milk replacer, weaned at 8 weeks.

C Reared by mother grazing outside.

KEY POINTS

- About 300 goats would be needed to provide a reasonable income from milk production.
- Very large numbers of fibre-producing goats would be required to provide a reasonable income from the sale of raw fibre.
- On a smaller scale it may be possible to generate enough income to pay for the upkeep of the goats.
- Adding value to milk can considerably increase the income, but processing equipment can be very expensive.
- Most people with small numbers of fibre-producing goats add value by using their mohair or cashmere to produce finished garments.

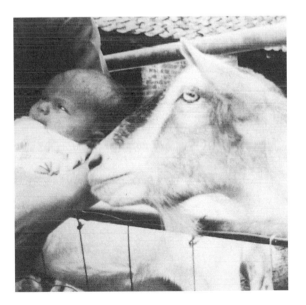

The pleasure of looking after these fascinating animals.

Chapter 8, goat meat is suitable for burgers, sausages and paté, and those with just a few goats may well find the sale of such products a profitable way of dealing with unwanted kids.

Whatever the level of interest, it has been shown in this chapter that there are possibilities for any goat keeper to develop a small business which may not be enough to support a family, but may well pay for the pleasure of looking after these fascinating animals.

Further Reading

BOOKS

Agricultural and Food Research Council, *The Nutrition of Goats* Technical Report No. 20 (CAB International, Wallingford, Oxon. CB11 3PL, 1998)

Dunn, P., *The Goatkeeper's Veterinary Book* 3rd ed. (Farming Press, Ipswich, 1994)

Hetherington, L., *All About Goats* 3rd ed. (Farming Press, Ipswich, 1992)

Mackenzie, D., *Goat Husbandry* 5th ed., revised and edited by Ruth Goodwin (Faber & Faber, London, 1993)

Matthews, J., *Diseases of the Goat* 2nd ed. (Blackwell Scientific Ltd, Oxford 1999)

Mowlem, A., *Goat Farming* 2nd ed. (Farming Press, Ipswich, 1992)

Peacock, C., *Improving Goat Production in the Tropics* (Oxfam/FARM–Africa 1996)

Porter, V., *Goats of the World* (Farming Press, Ipswich, 1996)

Webb, J. and Saunders, B., *Mohair – From Goat to Garment* (The Mohair Centre, Chiddingly, E. Sussex, 1992)

JOURNALS

British Goat Society, monthly journal (BGS, Bovey Tracey, Devon)

Country Smallholding magazine, Station Road, Newport, Saffron Walden, Essex

Smallholder magazine, High Street, Stoke Ferry, King's Lynn, Norfolk, PE33 9SF

Useful Addresses

UNITED KINGDOM

ADAS Consultancy Ltd
Oxford Spires Business Park
Kidlington
Oxford
OX5 1NZ

British Angora Goat Society
4th Street
National Agricultural Centre
Stoneleigh Park
Kenilworth
Warwickshire
CV8 2LG

British Goat Society
34–35 Fore Street
Bovey Tracey
Newton Abbot
Devon
TQ13 9AD

Goat Advisory Bureau
Water Farm Goat Centre Ltd
Stogursey
Bridgwater
Somerset
TA5 1PS

Goat Veterinary Society
Acorn House
25 Mardley Hill
Welwyn
Hertfordshire
AL6 0TT

Ministry of Agriculture, Fisheries & Food
3 Whitehall Place
London
SW1A 2HH

Rare Breeds Survival Trust
National Agricultural Centre
Stoneleigh Park
Kenilworth
Warwickshire
CV8 2LG

INTERNATIONAL

American Dairy Goat Association
PO Box 865
Spidal
NC 28160
USA

The American Meat Goat Association
P O Box 333
Junction
TX 76849-0333
USA

FARM-Africa
9–10 Southampton Place
Bloomsbury
London
WC1 2EA

Institut d'Elevage
149 rue de Bercy
75012 Paris
FRANCE

The International Goat Association
1015 Louisiana Street
Little Rock
AR 72202
USA

TEAGASC
Farranlea Road
Cork
Ireland

Index